Hey, Woman! Glow Up Your Life!

DARE TO LOVE YOURSELF, CRUSH DOUBT, AND STEP INTO YOUR POWER WITH POSITIVE AFFIRMATIONS

ZARA NIA IMANI

ACE EAST
PUBLISHING

Published by:

Ace East Publishing LLC

1401 21st Street, Suite R

Sacramento, CA 95811

ISBN: 978-1-963939-38-5

ASIN:

This is a work of nonfiction. The information contained in this book is based on the author's personal experiences and research and is intended for educational and informational purposes only. While the author and publisher have made every effort to ensure the accuracy of the information contained herein, this book should not be considered a substitute for professional advice. The reader assumes full responsibility for their use of this material.

For permissions, inquiries, or additional information, please contact:

Ace East Publishing at aceeast@aceeastpublishing.com

First Edition: 2025

Printed in the United States of America

Disclaimer

This book is intended for informational and motivational purposes only. The content is based on the author's personal experiences, research, and opinions and should not be considered professional, medical, psychological, or legal advice. Readers are encouraged to consult qualified professionals for specific advice tailored to their individual circumstances.

While every effort has been made to ensure the accuracy and completeness of the information contained within this book, the author and publisher make no guarantees or warranties, expressed or implied, regarding its applicability or effectiveness. The reader assumes full responsibility for any actions taken based on the material presented in this book.

The author and Ace East Publishing shall not be held liable for any damages, injuries, or losses that may arise from the use or misuse of this book's content.

This book is a tool for inspiration and self-reflection, and readers are encouraged to use it as part of a broader journey of personal growth and empowerment.

To every woman who has doubted her worth, questioned her strength, or felt the weight of the world on her shoulders—this book is for you.

May you rise with the confidence of a lioness, the strength of a warrior, and the resilience of a phoenix.

And to the women who have inspired generations to stand tall, fight for what's right, and believe in their own power—your light has guided us all.

To Rosa Parks, whose quiet courage sparked a revolution and reminded us that strength doesn't have to shout—it simply stands firm.

To Malala Yousafzai, who refused to be silenced and taught us that even the youngest voice can change the world.

To Maya Angelou, whose words continue to remind us that no matter the obstacles, we can rise and shine like the morning sun.

To Eleanor Roosevelt, who redefined what it means to lead with compassion and strength, proving that a woman's voice can change the course of history.

This book is a tribute to you and all women—may we always dare to dream bigger, love ourselves more fiercely, and step into our power.

With love and hope,

Contents

Introduction

Elena stands in front of the mirror, gripping the edges of the sink as if steadying herself for battle. Her reflection doesn't just stare back; it challenges her. 'Am I enough?' the question whispers in her mind, unspoken but deafening. For years, doubt had kept her small, but today, she decided to answer. She decides to break free from the chains of self-doubt that have held her back for too long.

This book is a wake-up call for her and for you. It's a declaration that the time has come to reclaim your power, love yourself unconditionally, and live your best life.

The vision for this book is simple yet profound: to empower you to shatter self-imposed limitations and embrace your full potential. Picture a butterfly emerging from its cocoon, vibrant and free, soaring into a sky of endless possibilities. This transformation is within your reach.

Let me share a piece of my journey with you. There was a time when doubt and fear followed me like shadows, always lurking, always whispering. I remember sitting in my car outside an interview I had worked so hard to land. My hands gripped the steering wheel as I rehearsed my introduction for the hundredth time, but the voice in my head wouldn't stop: 'What if they see through you? What if you fail?' I almost turned the key and drove away. That moment taught me something important: self-doubt doesn't just knock on your door; it builds a home in your mind if you let it. But through my struggles, I discovered strength and resilience I didn't know I had. This journey inspired me to help others do the same. I wrote this book because I believe in the incredible potential that lies within you.

This book is written for women who've ever felt the weight of self-doubt pressing down on their dreams, no matter where they are in life. Whether you're stepping into your first job, juggling the demands of a career and family, or rediscovering yourself after years of putting others first, this book is for you. It's for the perfectionist who feels she must always do more, the dreamer afraid to take that leap, and the woman who feels invisible in a crowded room. Wherever you are on your journey, know this: you are not alone. Self-doubt doesn't discriminate; it visits us all. But here's the good news: together, we can dismantle it. This book isn't here to tell you how to live; it's here to remind you of the strength you already possess and help you uncover the life you deserve.

So, what can you expect from this book? You'll learn how to silence self-doubt through powerful tools like journaling, affirmations, mindfulness, and cognitive restructuring. These techniques aren't just abstract ideas but practical, proven steps that help you break free and thrive. You'll gain the tools to design a life you love . . . a life that reflects your true self. These are not just promises; they are achievable outcomes that await you.

The book is structured to guide you from self-doubt to self-confidence. We'll start by exploring the roots of doubt and fear. Then, we'll move into strategies for building confidence and self-love. Each chapter is designed to build upon the last, creating a pathway to empowerment.

Now, I invite you to take the first step on this transformative journey. But before we can build a life of confidence and self-love, we must first face the invisible force that holds so many of us back: self-doubt. It whispers lies into our ears, telling us we aren't enough, that our dreams are out of reach, and that change is impossible. In Chapter 1, we'll name this inner voice for what it is: a saboteur. Together, we'll uncover its origins, challenge its lies, and reclaim the power it has stolen. This is the first step of your journey, a journey to rediscover the confident, capable woman you already are. Let's take it together. Turn the page, and let's begin.

Breaking Free from Self-Doubt

"No one can make you feel inferior without your consent."

ELEANOR ROOSEVELT

Perhaps you've been here before: sitting at your desk, your resume polished, your qualifications impeccable, yet an invisible barrier keeps you from hitting 'send.' That persistent whisper of doubt that you're not enough stops you cold. This inner voice, relentless and unforgiving, is all too familiar to many of us. It's the voice that questions your abilities and undermines your potential, casting shadows over your accomplishments and ambitions. This chapter invites you to recognize, confront, and ultimately silence this internal critic. By understanding its origins and learning to challenge its narrative, you'll reclaim the power to move forward with confidence and conviction.

PART 1 THE VOICE OF DOUBT: RECOGNIZING THE ENEMY WITHIN

Self-doubt often manifests as a pervasive, negative dialogue, an internal monologue that critiques and criticizes. This voice may appear during pivotal moments, like when you're preparing for an interview, and it whispers insidious thoughts of inadequacy, convincing you to self-sabotage. It might persuade you to decline opportunities, suggesting you're not ready or capable. Such doubt-driven decisions can keep you in a cycle of fear, preventing growth and progress.

The origins of this internal voice are varied and deeply rooted. Childhood experiences often lay the foundation for self-doubt. Perhaps you faced criticism from parents or authority figures, making you question your worth. Society also plays a significant role, with cultural pressures and beauty standards shaping self-esteem and adding layers to the voice's narrative. Fear of judgment becomes a formidable adversary, leading to internal conflicts and self-imposed limitations. Understanding these sources is crucial in dismantling the voice's hold over your life.

Identifying self-doubt requires awareness and reflection. Start with self-reflection journaling: dedicate time to writing down thoughts and feelings and recognizing patterns and triggers of self-doubt. Thought-tracking exercises can also illuminate how often negative beliefs surface, offering insights into their frequency and impact. Mindfulness meditation sessions, focusing on the present moment, can help observe thoughts without judgment, allowing you to see self-doubt for what it truly is . . . a fleeting construct of the mind, not an absolute truth.

For some, self-doubt stems from societal pressures, beauty standards, cultural expectations, or economic struggles that make us question our worth. These influences are often compounded by race, class, or background, creating layers of self-imposed limitations. By recognizing how these forces shape our inner voice, we can begin to challenge and dismantle them.

Once you've identified these doubts, confronting and questioning them is the next step. Cognitive restructuring techniques, a cornerstone of Cognitive Behavioral Therapy, offer effective methods for challenging and reframing negative thoughts. This involves examining the validity and logic of these beliefs through structured questioning. Ask yourself, "Is this thought based on fact?" or "What evidence supports this belief?" You reduce its power and influence by systematically dismantling the assumptions behind self-doubt.

Empowering yourself through positive self-questioning is another strategy. Replace doubt with affirmations that affirm your capabilities and potential. Remind yourself of past successes and strengths, reinforcing a narrative of competence and achievement. This proactive questioning shifts the view from limitations to possibilities, helping you cultivate a mindset of resilience and self-assurance.

The Voice of Doubt: Recognizing the Enemy Within

Spend a few minutes each day reflecting on moments when self-doubt appears. Write them down, noting the situation, thoughts, and emotions involved. Ask yourself, "What triggered this doubt?" and "Is there an alternative perspective?" Use this exercise to build awareness and begin the journey of transforming doubt into confidence.

PART 2 UNCOVERING LIMITING BELIEFS: THE ROOTS OF SELF-DOUBT

Limiting beliefs are the invisible chains that bind us, whispering deceitful truths about our potential and self-worth. These profoundly ingrained convictions often echo phrases like "I am not good enough" or "I don't deserve success," statements that can shape the trajectory of our lives if left unchallenged. Such beliefs are not mere thoughts but powerful narratives that confine our aspirations and fuel persistent self-doubt. They operate like a silent script, dictating our actions and decisions, often steering us away from opportunities and growth. Recognizing these beliefs is the first step towards liberation, as they often masquerade as truth, subtly influencing our choices and interactions.

To uncover these limiting beliefs, one must engage in introspective exploration. Visualization exercises can be a potent tool, allowing you to envision a life unencumbered by these constraints. Close your eyes and see yourself achieving your goals without the weight of doubt. What does that success look like? Who are you in that scenario? This exercise helps identify the beliefs that stand in your way. Guided introspection sessions can also be valuable, encouraging you to trace these beliefs back to their origin. Reflect on past experiences that may have seeded these thoughts. Was there a moment or repeated message that planted the idea of inadequacy? By understanding their roots, you can begin to dismantle their influence.

The consequences of leaving these beliefs unchallenged can be profound. They often lead to missed opportunities and stunted personal growth. Consider the case of a talented writer who never submits her work for fear it won't be well-received. Her belief that she's not good enough confines her potential, denying her the chance to share her talent and grow from feedback. This self-imposed limitation keeps her in a cycle of stagnation, where potential remains untapped. Real-life examples abound, illustrating how accepting these beliefs can hold us back in career advancements, personal relationships, and self-fulfillment.

Challenging and reframing limiting beliefs is a transformative process. Begin with affirmative counterstatements. For every negative belief, create a positive alternative. Replace "I am not good enough" with "I am capable and deserving of success." These statements should resonate with your truth, reinforcing a new narrative that supports your growth. Role-playing positive outcomes can also help in altering these beliefs. Envision a situation where you succeed despite your doubts and rehearse how that success feels and looks. This practice not only builds confidence but also prepares your mind to accept and embrace new possibilities.

By addressing and altering limiting beliefs, you empower yourself to break free from the confines of self-doubt. This shift opens doors to opportunities and growth, allowing you to step into a life where the potential is realized, and dreams are pursued without hesitation.

PART 3 FROM SELF-DOUBT TO SELF-BELIEF: CRAFTING EMPOWERING AFFIRMATIONS

Yes, the power of words is not just as tools for communication but as catalysts for change. Affirmations are a potent instrument in transforming self-doubt into self-belief. They work by reshaping the brain's response to negative thoughts through repetition. This phenomenon is rooted in neuroplasticity, the brain's remarkable ability to rewire and form new neural pathways. By consistently feeding your mind positive affirmations, you can weaken the grip of doubt and nurture a mindset of confidence. Each affirmation you repeat is like a stroke of a brush on the canvas of your mind, painting an avatar of self-assurance and potential.

Creating effective affirmations is about resonance and authenticity. They must reflect your deepest goals and values. Start with "I am" statements that speak directly to your aspirations. For instance, "I am capable of achieving my dreams" or "I am worthy of love and respect." These phrases should evoke a strong emotional response, stirring something within you that feels both inspiring and true. When an affirmation resonates emotionally, it becomes more than just words . . . it becomes a part of your belief system, gradually shifting your mindset towards positivity and empowerment.

Incorporating affirmations into your daily routine can maximize their impact. Begin with morning rituals; as you wake, repeat your affirmations aloud, setting a positive tone for the day. In the evening, reflect on them again, reinforcing your beliefs before sleep. An affirmation journal can also be a valuable tool, where you write down your affirmations and reflect on their meaning. Technology offers another avenue: using apps that send reminders or record your affirmations in your voice, playing them back to reinforce your commitment. These practices anchor affirmations in your daily life, creating a steady rhythm of positivity.

Reflect on the story of Angela, a talented graphic designer who constantly felt like she was one mistake away from being exposed as a fraud. Her work had won awards, and clients raved about her creativity, but every time she submitted a project, she braced for criticism. When her boss called her a 'genius' after a presentation, she dismissed it, thinking, 'He's just being nice.' At night, her inner voice whispered: 'You just got lucky. They'll figure it out soon.'

One day, Angela decided she was tired of living under the shadow of self-doubt. She began a simple daily practice: standing in front of her mirror, she said aloud, 'I am talented. My work has an impact. I am enough.' At first, the words felt hollow, like repeating a script she didn't believe. But she stuck with it, pairing the affirmations with a journal where she documented her successes each day, no matter how small. 'Met a tough deadline' or 'Client loved the design' became evidence that began to silence her doubts.

Six months later, something shifted. When a colleague praised her work during a meeting, she smiled and said, 'Thank you,' without mentally discounting it. She even volunteered to lead a high-stakes project, a role she would have declined before. Angela wasn't just doing good work anymore; she believed in her ability to do great work. Her affirmations didn't just change the way she spoke to herself; they changed the way she showed up in the world.

Each affirmation you repeat is like a screenshot of a work of art in your mind, creating a projection of self-assurance and potential. Affirmations are not just a practice but a lifestyle choice. They require commitment and consistency, like tending to a plot of soil that, with time, will bloom. Embrace them as part of your daily rhythm, allowing them to cultivate a space in your mind where self-doubt has no room to grow. Through this practice, you will find that affirmations are not just words but seeds of empowerment, rooting themselves in your consciousness and nurturing the growth of a more confident, assured self.

PART 4 SUCCESS STORIES: TRANSFORMATIONS FROM DOUBT TO CONFIDENCE

In a bustling city, Sandra found herself at a crossroads in her career. Her job, although stable, left her feeling unfulfilled and burdened by a constant sense of doubt. The familiar voice of uncertainty whispered that a change was too risky, telling her she wasn't skilled enough to start over. Yet, something inside pushed her to reconsider. One day, after another sleepless night, she realized the idea of staying where she was and felt far more frightened than taking a leap into the unknown.

She decided to pivot from her corporate role to pursue a passion for sustainable fashion, a field that aligned with her values but required stepping entirely out of her comfort zone. The transition was daunting. In the early days, Sandra struggled with financial uncertainty, rejection from potential collaborators, and nagging self-doubt that crept in at every misstep. There were moments when she almost gave up, asking herself, 'What if I fail?' But instead of letting these fears define her, she leaned into consistent self-reflection, journaling her challenges and reframing them as opportunities to learn and grow.

Gradually, her persistence paid off. Sandra built a network of like-minded individuals who shared her vision, attending events, joining online forums, and reaching out to mentors in the industry. This community became her sounding board, offering encouragement, sharing resources, and helping her see what she couldn't always see in herself. Over time, Sandra's confidence grew, and she began to trust not only her abilities but her instincts. Today, Sandra leads her sustainable fashion initiative, using her story to inspire others to chase their dreams. Her journey is a testament to what can happen when we trust in our abilities, embrace self-reflection, and lean on a supportive community.

In another part of the world, a young woman, Silvia, embarked on a deeply personal transformation, confronting years of negative self-image and body dissatisfaction. For as long as she could remember, Silvia felt defined by society's harsh standards of beauty, always too much of this or not enough of that. These judgments left her feeling invisible, unworthy, and trapped in a cycle of self-doubt and shame. Every time she looked in the mirror, she saw a reflection shaped by others' expectations, not her truth.

One day, Silvia decided she was tired of feeling like a prisoner in her own skin. She committed to challenging these perceptions, embarking on a journey toward body positivity. The shift began with small, intentional changes. She stopped following social media accounts that made her feel inadequate and replaced them with ones that celebrated diversity and authenticity. Sylvia immersed herself in communities that championed inclusivity, attending local body positivity meetups and online forums where people shared their stories. These spaces became her lifeline, a safe haven where she could share her own struggles and, for the first time, receive affirmation without judgment.

Her journey was not without setbacks. There were days when old habits and doubts resurfaced, whispering that she would never truly accept herself. But Silvia remained steadfast. She practiced self-compassion, reminding herself that change is a process, not an overnight transformation. Slowly, she began to document her progress. She started taking photographs, not to hide behind filters but to tell her story honestly. Through this practice, she reframed her narrative, seeing her body not as a source of shame but as a vessel of strength and resilience.

Silvia's story is a testament to the power of self-acceptance and community in overcoming deep-seated insecurities. Her transformation wasn't about achieving perfection; it was about rewriting her relationship with her body and embracing her inherent worth. Through courage and support, Silvia redefined her identity, proving that it's possible to create a narrative of pride and self-love.

Both Sandra and Silvia leaned on common tools to navigate their journeys: consistent self-reflection, a growth mindset, and the unwavering support of a community. These strategies became the bedrock of their transformations, offering them strength and clarity when doubt threatened to take over.

These narratives remind us that overcoming self-doubt is universally achievable. Despite their differing circumstances, Sandra and Silvia's journeys highlight the themes of resilience and determination. They prove that transformation is possible when we commit to change, embrace support, and view setbacks not as failures but as lessons along the way.

As you read these stories, contemplate how they resonate with your own experiences. What moments of doubt in your life mirror Sandra's or Silvia's journeys? Reflect on the aspects of their stories that speak to you: Is there a passion you've been afraid to pursue? Do you feel trapped by unrealistic standards or expectations?

Now, take a moment to write down your thoughts. Use these questions as prompts to explore your own transformation:

- What area of your life feels weighed down by doubt?
- What small, intentional steps could you take today to challenge that doubt?
- Who or what could offer the support you need to move forward?

As you reflect, remember that transformation begins with a single step. Let Sandra and Silvia remind you of a simple truth: the power to transform your life has always been within you. It's time to take the first step, trust yourself, and create the future you deserve.

PART 5 SELF-REFLECTION EXERCISES: IDENTIFYING AND OVERCOMING TRIGGERS

Have you ever walked into a meeting or opened your social media feed only to feel a sudden wave of self-doubt? These moments often seem random, but they're not. Self-doubt has triggers, hidden cues that shape our thoughts and behaviors, often without us even realizing it. Through self-reflection, we can peel back the layers of our minds, uncovering these triggers and reclaiming control over our narrative. This process is more than introspection; it's about becoming a detective of your inner world and observing patterns with curiosity instead of judgment.

One effective method for this exploration is maintaining a trigger journal. This simple yet powerful tool involves jotting down situations, people, or emotions that spark feelings of inadequacy. For example, you might notice that after scrolling through a particular social media platform, you feel anxious or compare yourself to others. Or perhaps a recurring pattern emerges, like feeling self-doubt whenever you're in a meeting with a critical colleague. By capturing these moments, the journal transforms vague unease into tangible insights, helping you identify recurring triggers and understand their impact.

Through emotional mapping, we delve deeper, linking feelings to specific events and creating a visual representation of how and when doubt manifests. For example, let's say you reflect on a recent work meeting where you felt dismissed. In your chart, you might write:

- **Situation:** Weekly team meeting.
- **Emotion:** Anxiety, frustration, self-doubt.
- **Trigger:** A colleague's dismissive tone when responding to my ideas.

As you continue mapping, you may notice patterns; for instance, certain individuals, environments, or situations consistently evoke these feelings. These insights not only highlight triggers but also offer a roadmap for addressing them.

With these insights, strategies for addressing and mitigating triggers come into sharp view. One such strategy is exposure therapy, a technique often used in behavioral psychology. It involves gradually confronting fear-inducing situations in a controlled, manageable way. For example, if public speaking triggers self-doubt, begin with a trickle by practicing in front of a loyal companion or family member, then gradually increase the audience size. Each step might feel uncomfortable at first but remember: growth happens in a space just outside your comfort zone. By taking small, intentional steps, you diminish the power of fear, building resilience and confidence over time.

Another strategy is reframing experiences. Challenges, often seen as threats, can be viewed instead as opportunities for growth. For instance, let's say you receive constructive criticism at work. Instead of internalizing it as evidence of failure, you can reframe it as a chance to improve your skills and showcase your resilience. This shift in perspective transforms anxiety into empowerment, turning obstacles into accessible paths to enlightenment.

Ongoing self-assessment is vital. It's easy to slip back into old habits, so regular check-ins with yourself help maintain the progress you've made. Set aside time weekly or monthly to review your trigger journal and emotional map. Celebrate your wins, no matter how small, and adjust strategies as needed. Remember: self-awareness is an evolving practice, not a static achievement. Each small step forward strengthens your foundation, proving that change is possible. The more you understand yourself, the more you'll find that self-doubt doesn't define you; it's simply a whisper you've learned to quiet.

Interactive Element: Emotional Mapping Exercise

Create an emotional map by drawing a chart with three columns: Situations, Emotions, and Triggers. In the first column, list specific situations or events from the past week. In the second, write down the emotions you felt during each situation, whether it was anxiety, frustration, or doubt. Finally, in the third column, identify the triggers linked to these emotions.

Here's an example:

- **Situation:** Feedback meeting at work.
- **Emotion:** Self-doubt, defensiveness.
- **Trigger:** Feeling unprepared after receiving unexpected constructive criticism.

Once your map is complete, review it to look for patterns or recurring themes. Are there specific environments or people that trigger doubt more often? Use this map as a tool to guide your growth, helping you develop strategies to address these triggers and move forward with confidence.

PART 6 BUILDING A FOUNDATION: DEVELOPING UNWAVERING SELF-CONFIDENCE

Self-confidence is not a one-size-fits-all attribute; it's more like a green retreat that requires time, care, and the right tools to thrive. At its core, there are three essential elements: self-efficacy, self-worth, and resilience. These are the seeds that, when nurtured, grow into a foundation of genuine confidence. Each element plays a unique role: self-efficacy is the belief that you can achieve your goals, self-worth is the intrinsic value you place on yourself, and resilience is the ability to bounce back when life throws challenges your way. Together, these components form the bedrock of confidence, enabling you to build a life of purpose and fulfillment.

Growing your self-confidence requires deliberate practice and commitment. One powerful way to nurture it is through skill-building activities. Engage in learning new competencies, whether it's mastering a professional skill like public speaking, trying a new creative hobby like painting, or tackling a physical challenge like running a 5K. Each new skill mastered adds a layer to your self-assurance, proving to yourself that you can tackle challenges and succeed. For example, learning to cook a new dish might seem small, but the confidence it brings, 'I tried something new and succeeded,' can ripple into other areas of your life. This process isn't just about acquiring knowledge; it's about reinforcing your ability to learn, adapt, and grow.

Resilience plays a pivotal role in maintaining confidence; it's the armor that protects you when life throws curveballs your way. Building resilience involves training your mind to view setbacks not as failures but as lessons. For example, think of Serena, an entrepreneur who launched her dream business only to face financial struggles in the first year. At first, she felt defeated, but instead of giving up, she reflected on what went wrong and sought advice from mentors. She adjusted her strategy, learned from her mistakes, and eventually grew her business into a thriving success. Her story shows how perseverance and a willingness to learn can transform setbacks into opportunities for growth.

Adopting a growth-oriented mindset is another key to building confidence. This mindset champions the idea that learning never ceases and that each challenge is an opportunity for personal development. Cultivate this mindset by using affirmations focused on growth, such as:

- 'I am capable of learning and improving.'
- 'I learn from every experience, no matter the outcome.'
- 'Setbacks are temporary; I grow stronger with each challenge.'

To maximize their impact, repeat these affirmations daily, whether as part of a morning routine, before tackling a difficult task, or whenever doubt creeps in. Over time, these words will reshape your inner dialogue, reinforcing the belief that you are capable of evolving and improving, no matter the circumstances.

As you cultivate these aspects of confidence, remember that it's a continuous process. Confidence is not a destination but a way of living, requiring consistent nurturing and attention. Think of it as a compass that guides you through life's myriad challenges, pointing you toward your true potential. Allow yourself the grace to grow and evolve, knowing that each day presents a new opportunity to strengthen your foundation. With this unwavering confidence, the world opens up in ways you never imagined, inviting you to embrace the life you've always dreamed of. So, take that first step today, trusting in your power to move forward with courage and purpose. You are enough.

CHAPTER 2

Cultivating Authenticity and Vulnerability

> "Authenticity is the daily practice of letting go of who we think we're supposed to be and embracing who we are."
>
> *BRENE' BROWN*

In a chatter-filled Starbucks, a woman, Janis, sits with a notebook open before her, pen poised above the page. The air around her hums with the sounds of milk steaming, orders being called out, and quiet conversations, but Janis is lost in her own world. Her mind is a whirlwind of thoughts and emotions, yet what she yearns for most is clarity. She hesitates before writing the first word, afraid that what she puts on the page will reveal truths she's not ready to face. But as the ink begins to flow, so do her thoughts. She writes about who she is, who she's pretending to be, and who she longs to become. For the first time, she acknowledges the disconnect between her actions and her values. This journey to authenticity, she realizes, is not a straight path; it's a series of revelations and reckonings, where each step brings her closer to her true self. Janis understands that living authentically is about more than just being honest with others; it's about being honest with herself, aligning her actions with her deepest values, and embracing who she truly is without shame or pretense.

Authenticity is the practice of living in alignment with one's true self, a state of congruence that brings profound fulfillment and self-awareness. It is about embodying honesty and integrity, not only in your interactions with others but also in your relationship with yourself. Living authentically means acknowledging your strengths and weaknesses, embracing your quirks and imperfections, and being unafraid to show the world who you are. It is the courage to stand firm in your beliefs and values, even when they diverge from those around you. This alignment with your inner truth allows for a life that is not only fulfilling but also rich in purpose and meaning.

Yet, the path to authenticity is often fraught with obstacles. Societal expectations can act as formidable barriers, pressuring individuals to conform to established norms and ideals. For instance, ponder a young professional named Ethan, who felt compelled to pursue a corporate career because it was expected of him by his family. While outwardly successful, he felt increasingly disconnected from his creative passions. This disconnect led to frustration and a sense of living someone else's life. Like many, Ethan faced the fear of rejection and judgment; what would his family think if he left his stable job to pursue art? For years, the perceived threat of isolation and failure kept him in a cycle of conformity. Ethan's story highlights how these pressures can suppress personal desires and values, keeping individuals from living authentically.

Identifying one's core values is a foundational step towards living authentically. These values act as a compass, guiding decisions and actions in a way that feels true and right. To uncover these values, engage in a core values assessment. Reflect on moments in life when you felt most fulfilled; what values were you honoring at those times? Conversely, think about times of dissatisfaction or conflict. What values were being compromised? Another powerful tool is the creation of a personal mission statement. This statement serves as a declaration of intent, encapsulating what you stand for and what you hope to achieve. To craft your own mission statement, start by reflecting on your core values and asking yourself:

- "What do I want to contribute to the world?"
- "What principles do I want to live by?"
- "What legacy do I want to leave behind?"

Your mission statement doesn't have to be perfect or lengthy. For example, it might be as simple as: "To live a life of curiosity, compassion, and creativity, and to inspire others to do the same." This statement can become a source of motivation and clarity, reminding you of your purpose and guiding your decisions.

Aligning your actions with your core values requires intentionality and courage. It involves making choices that reflect your beliefs, even when they are unpopular or challenging. Value-based decision-making is an essential practice in this alignment. Before making a decision, pause and ask yourself: "Does this choice reflect my values? Does it bring me closer to the person I want to be?" This practice ensures that your actions are not only authentic but also constructive, leading to a life of integrity and coherence. Lifestyle adjustments may also be necessary to maintain congruence. This might mean reevaluating relationships, career paths, or habits that no longer serve your authentic self. Such changes can be daunting, but they are essential for living a life that is true to who you are.

Exercise: Core Values Discovery

Take a moment to sit quietly and reflect on your core values. Write down five values that are most important to you. These might include values like honesty, kindness, creativity, or independence. If you're unsure where to start, think about moments in your life when you felt most fulfilled. What values were you honoring at those times? Conversely, think about times of dissatisfaction or conflict . . . what values were being compromised? Once you've identified your values, reflect on how they influence your daily decisions and actions. Are there areas of your life where you feel misaligned with these values? For example, if independence is a core value, are you in a relationship or job that stifles your autonomy? What changes can you make to better align your life with your authentic self? This exercise is not about perfection but about gaining clarity and direction, helping you live more authentically each day.

By embracing authenticity, you embark on a journey of self-discovery and empowerment. Each step forward is like peeling back layers of an onion, revealing more of your true self beneath. The road may not always be easy, but it is one worth traveling. Living authentically is a gift you give yourself, a declaration that your voice, your values, and your unique presence in the world matter. With every choice aligned to your truth, you take a step closer to living a life that is truly your own.

PART 1 VULNERABILITY AS STRENGTH: REDEFINING WEAKNESS

Envision standing before a group, your heart pounding as your palms grow damp with sweat. You glance at the expectant faces staring back at you, your voice trembling as you begin to share a personal story that reveals your deepest fears. For a moment, the urge to retreat overwhelms you, but you press on. With every word, you feel the weightlifting from your chest, the room leaning in closer as your honesty resonates. This act, though terrifying, is a testament to true strength. Vulnerability is often seen as a weakness, a crack in the armor that leaves you exposed to judgment and harm. But in truth, it is a courageous act that fosters personal and relational growth.

In leadership, for example, vulnerability fosters trust and connection. Leaders who acknowledge their own limitations and uncertainties inspire loyalty and respect, creating environments where others feel safe to express themselves. This openness is not a sign of fragility but a bold statement of authenticity and strength.

Embracing vulnerability can transform relationships, deepen emotional intimacy, and foster empathy. When you allow yourself to be seen without pretense, you invite others to do the same, creating bonds built on trust and understanding. Relationships flourish when both parties are willing to share their truths, fears, and dreams. This openness enhances resilience, as it encourages a culture where mistakes are learning opportunities rather than failures. By being vulnerable, you acknowledge that you're human, capable of both success and error. This acceptance strengthens your ability to adapt and grow, as it frees you from the pressure of perfection. Think of vulnerability as a tree swaying in the wind. While its branches may bend under the force of a storm, its roots grow deeper, anchoring it more firmly in the earth. Similarly, embracing vulnerability allows you to weather life's challenges with greater resilience, knowing that openness is a source of strength rather than weakness.

Practicing vulnerability requires intentionality and gradual steps. Start by sharing personal stories within trusted circles, where empathy and understanding prevail. These stories don't have to be grand revelations; they can be simple admissions of everyday struggles or fears. The act of sharing is what matters. As you open up, practice active listening and empathy, both for yourself and others. Listen not to respond but to understand, fostering a space where vulnerability is welcomed, not judged. This creates a ripple effect, encouraging others to share and connect on a deeper level. Vulnerability becomes a shared journey, enriching all involved.

Practicing vulnerability doesn't mean exposing every detail of your life to everyone. It's about choosing when, where, and with whom to share your authentic self. For example, a manager might admit to their team, "I made a mistake in this project, but here's how I'm learning from it," fostering trust and openness in a professional context. In contrast, deeply personal struggles might be reserved for a steadfast ally or therapist. The strength of vulnerability lies in this discernment. Openness paired with self-awareness and boundaries ensures that sharing remains an act of courage rather than a source of harm.

As vulnerability fosters deeper connections and self-awareness, it naturally paves the way for authentic expression. The courage to reveal your true self, your fears, dreams, and imperfections creates a foundation for expressing your voice in a way that feels genuine and impactful.

PART 2 AUTHENTIC EXPRESSION: FINDING YOUR VOICE IN A NOISY WORLD

Visualize a singer stepping onto a dimly lit stage, her voice a gentle whisper that gradually rises to fill the room. This is the power of authentic expression, finding and using your voice in a world that often seems too loud. Authentic expression is more than just speaking; it's about allowing your true self to be heard and felt. When you express yourself authentically, you not only affirm your own identity but also empower yourself and influence those around you. This act of self-expression boosts self-esteem because it affirms that your perspective matters. It validates your thoughts and emotions, reinforcing a sense of self-worth and confidence. By articulating what you truly feel and believe, you assert your place in the world, creating ripples that inspire change and connection.

Yet, amidst the cacophony of opinions and expectations, staying true to oneself is no easy feat. With its curated images and high-light reels, social media presents an endless parade of perfection, beaming smiles, flawless vacations, and success stories stripped of struggle. Scrolling through this polished reality, you might find yourself asking, "Am I enough?" Similarly, peer pressure can feel like a relentless tide, pushing you to mold your identity to fit group norms. Whether it's laughing at a joke that doesn't align with your values or suppressing your dreams to avoid standing out, these pressures can silence your voice and create a disconnect between who you are and who you present to the world.

To cultivate authentic expression, assess engaging with creative outlets such as writing, art, or music. For instance, Mitzi struggled to articulate her emotions after a difficult breakup. Turning to art, she began painting abstract pieces that reflected her inner turmoil, swirling blues for sadness and fiery reds for anger. Over time, her canvases evolved into expressions of hope and healing. Whether through painting, writing, or music, creative outlets offer a safe space for self-expression, where vulnerability transforms into empowerment.

Though daunting for some, public speaking is another avenue where authenticity can shine. When you speak from the heart, your words carry weight and sincerity, resonating with listeners who connect to your passion and truth. Experimentation is key to finding what form of expression resonates best with you. Try different mediums like blogs or podcasts, where you can explore topics that matter to you. Blogging offers a platform to share your insights and experiences, while podcasts allow for a more conversational exploration of ideas. Journaling prompts can also guide you in this exploration, encouraging self-discovery and reflection. Questions like "What do I want to say to the world?" or "How do I feel when I'm genuinely expressing myself?" can reveal deeper insights into your authentic self.

Embracing vulnerability and finding your authentic voice is not an overnight transformation. It's a journey of small, courageous steps. Start today. Share a piece of your story with someone you trust. Write a journal entry where you pour your heart onto the page. Sing, paint, or speak without worrying about perfection. Each act of openness is a step toward a life where your true self is seen, heard, and celebrated. Remember: your voice matters, and the world needs the light only you can bring.

Interactive Element: Journaling Prompts for Authentic Expression

1. Reflect on a moment when you felt truly heard and seen. What were you expressing, and how did it feel?
2. Write about a topic or issue you are passionate about. Why does it matter to you, and how can you express this passion authentically?

3. You are about to give a speech to the world. What message would you want to convey?

These prompts are designed to help you explore and refine your authentic voice, encouraging a deeper connection with yourself and others.

PART 3 REAL-LIFE NARRATIVES: STORIES OF COURAGEOUS VULNERABILITY

Now, here is Trudy, a professional woman who spent years hiding behind a mask of perfection, believing that showing any vulnerability would lead to shame and rejection. Growing up in an environment where emotional strength was equated with stoicism, she learned early to shield her true feelings. However, an unexpected life event shattered this facade, forcing her to confront her hidden shame. In a moment of courage, she decided to share her story with a close friend. What she discovered was not judgment but compassion and understanding. This act of vulnerability opened doors she never imagined, leading to deeper connections and a liberation she had long suppressed. She found strength not in hiding her shame but in embracing and sharing it, allowing her relationships to flourish and her personal growth to accelerate. This transformation illustrates how vulnerability can indeed become a source of power.

Review the story of Nancy, a City Councilwoman who bravely decided to reveal personal struggles with mental health despite the risks of public scrutiny. This revelation was a bold move in an industry that often values image over authenticity. Yet, it sparked a dialogue that reached thousands, offering solace to many who felt alone in their struggles. Her openness not only humanized her but also inspired countless others to seek help and embrace their own vulnerabilities. Through this act, she transformed a perceived weakness into an opportunity for leadership and advocacy, advancing her career in unexpected ways. Her story demonstrates how vulnerability can dismantle barriers and foster a sense of community and belonging.

These narratives underscore significant outcomes that can arise from embracing vulnerability. One profound impact is the reconciliation that can occur within families through open communication. When individuals allow themselves to be vulnerable, they create spaces for honesty and healing, bridging gaps that may have seemed insurmountable. By sharing fears and emotions openly, family members can find common ground and understanding, leading to strengthened bonds and renewed connections. Similarly, in professional settings, authentic leadership, rooted in vulnerability, can pave the way for career advancement. When leaders show their human side, acknowledging mistakes and uncertainties, they foster trust and loyalty, cultivating environments where innovation and collaboration thrive. This approach not only enhances team dynamics but also positions leaders as relatable and inspiring.

The lessons from these stories are clear and applicable in everyday life. Trusting the process, even when the outcome is uncertain, is a vital part of embracing vulnerability. It requires faith that revealing your true self will lead to growth and positive change, even if the path is unclear. Additionally, these stories highlight the immense value of supportive networks. Surrounding yourself with people who encourage and affirm your vulnerability creates a safety net, allowing you to take risks and grow. These networks can provide the strength and encouragement needed to face challenges, reinforcing the idea that vulnerability is not a solitary endeavor but a shared experience that connects us all.

Take a moment to reflect on your own story. Weigh those instances where you have shown vulnerability and the impact it had on your life. What have you learned about yourself through these experiences? What strengths did you uncover? Reflecting on your own narrative can provide insights into how vulnerability has shaped your journey and reveal areas where you can continue to grow and connect with others. By embracing your own story, you can unlock the power of vulnerability, transforming fear into courage and isolation into connection.

PART 4 SELF-REFLECTION PROMPTS FOR AUTHENTIC LIVING

Self-reflection is like cleaning out a long-forgotten drawer. At first, it may seem daunting or even messy, but as you sort through the clutter, you uncover hidden treasures, pieces of yourself you had forgotten or never fully understood. It's a powerful tool that allows you to peel back the layers of your consciousness, revealing the core of who you truly are. In a world that demands constant motion, self-reflection creates a rare moment of stillness, where you can tune out the external noise and listen to the whispers of your inner self. Through this process, you gain clarity about your desires, fears, and motivations, aligning your life with your deepest values. This alignment brings a sense of purpose and fulfillment, allowing you to live with integrity and authenticity.

To guide you on this path of self-discovery, examine these specific prompts that can illuminate your inner landscape:

- **What does authenticity mean to me?** For some, authenticity might mean having the courage to express unpopular opinions in a group setting. For others, it could mean living a life that prioritizes creativity, family, or adventure. Take time to reflect on how your personal definition of authenticity shapes your daily decisions.

- **How do I express my true self?** Do you share your thoughts openly, or do you hold back out of fear of judgment? Do you express your identity through creative outlets, such as art or writing, or in smaller, everyday ways, like the way you dress or decorate your home?
- **What fears hold me back from being authentic?** Fear often comes disguised as self-doubt or the need for external validation. Perhaps you worry about rejection from loved ones or judgment from peers. Identifying these fears is the first step toward dismantling their power.

Regular self-reflection is not a one-time exercise but a continuous practice that deepens over time. Establishing a routine for this introspection can help maintain your authenticity. Set aside time each week to reflect on your experiences, thoughts, and emotions. This can be through writing in a reflection journal, where you document your insights and growth, or through quiet contemplation, where you simply sit with your thoughts. Consistency is key, as regular reflection allows you to track your progress, notice patterns, and adjust your actions accordingly. It creates a rhythm of introspection that becomes a natural part of your life, supporting your ongoing journey of self-discovery and authenticity.

The impact of self-reflection on personal growth is profound. Analyze the story of Maria, a marketing executive who felt an unshakable sense of dissatisfaction with her career. Through regular self-reflection, Maria began asking herself hard questions: "What truly brings me joy?" and "Why does this job feel empty despite its rewards?" Over time, she uncovered a passion for helping others and eventually transitioned into a counseling career. The process wasn't easy. Maria grappled with fear and self-doubt, but her introspection gave her the clarity and courage to pursue a life that resonated with her true self.

Similarly, Rebecca used self-reflection to overcome self-doubt and cultivate self-compassion. During her weekly reflection sessions, she noticed negative patterns in her inner dialogue, such as words like "failure" and "not good enough." By replacing these phrases with positive affirmations, such as "I'm learning" and "I deserve kindness," she transformed her self-esteem and strengthened her confidence.

Interactive Element: Weekly Reflection Routine

Establish a weekly reflection routine to deepen your understanding of yourself. Dedicate 30 minutes each week to sit quietly with your thoughts or write in a journal. Begin by answering these prompts:

1. **What were the highlights of my week, and what do they reveal about my values?**
2. **Did I encounter any challenges, and how did I respond authentically?**
3. **What can I learn from my experiences this week to live more in alignment with my true self?**

You can adapt this routine to fit your needs. Some weeks, you might concentrate on gratitude, while others might center around identifying areas for personal growth. The key is consistency. By creating a rhythm of introspection, you cultivate a habit of tuning into your inner self, nurturing a life that is truly your own.

By making self-reflection a regular practice, you open the door to profound growth and clarity. Take that first step today: set aside 10 minutes to sit quietly, pick up a journal, and ask yourself one of the prompts above. Even a small act of introspection can spark transformation, guiding you toward a life that feels aligned, intentional, and authentically yours.

PART 5 TECHNIQUES FOR OVERCOMING FEAR OF JUDGMENT

Fear of judgment can cast a long shadow over our lives, often inhibiting us from living authentically. Bring to mind standing on stage with a spotlight illuminating your face as dozens of eyes fixed on you. Your heart pounds, your palms sweat, and your voice catches in your throat. You open your mouth to speak, but instead of words, doubts flood your mind: *What if they don't like what I say? What if I make a fool of myself?* The weight of perceived judgment feels suffocating, freezing you in place. This judgment-induced anxiety can be paralyzing, making you second-guess your choices and suppress your authentic voice. Over time, it becomes a barrier, preventing you from pursuing your passions or even speaking up, trapping you in a cycle of self-censorship and inauthenticity.

To combat this pervasive fear, cognitive behavioral techniques offer powerful tools for reframing negative thoughts. Begin by identifying the specific idea that's causing anxiety. For instance, if you're worried about speaking up in a meeting, you might think, *If I say something wrong, everyone will judge me.* Challenge this thought by asking, *What evidence do I have that this will happen? Have I spoken up before, and what was the outcome?* Often, you'll find that the fear is exaggerated. Replace the negative thought with a more constructive affirmation, such as, *My input is valuable, and even if I make a mistake, it's an opportunity to learn.* Over time, this practice trains your mind to approach situations with greater clarity and confidence.

Assertiveness training is another effective way to overcome the fear of judgment. This involves learning to communicate your needs and boundaries clearly and respectfully. Start with small steps, such as saying 'no' to minor requests that don't align with your priorities. For example, if a colleague asks you to take on extra work you don't have time for, respond with, 'I appreciate you thinking of me, but I'm unable to take on additional tasks right now.' Practicing these moments of assertiveness builds your confidence over time, affirming that your voice and needs matter just as much as anyone else's.

Creating a supportive environment is equally important. Surround yourself with individuals who celebrate your true self, not those who stifle it. For example, join a book club or creative group where open dialogue and diverse perspectives are encouraged. If your immediate circle feels unsupportive, seek out communities online or in person where shared interests foster connection. Safe spaces, like mindfulness workshops or mental health support groups, can offer havens where you can express yourself without fear of judgment. These environments remind you that authenticity isn't just accepted; it's valued.

Promoting self-validation over external validation is another vital step. Shift the aim inward, prioritizing your self-approval and understanding that your happiness and fulfillment are not dependent on others' opinions. For instance, think about a time when you accomplished something meaningful but didn't receive recognition. Instead of waiting for others to notice, take a moment to acknowledge your effort. You might say to yourself, *I worked hard on this, and I'm proud of what I achieved.* Pairing this practice with daily affirmations, such as, *I am enough,* or *others' opinions don't define My worth,* helps cultivate an inner sense of security and self-respect.

Overcoming the fear of judgment is like learning to walk on a tightrope; you may wobble at first, but with practice, you'll find your balance. Each step forward is an act of courage, a declaration that your voice and truth matter. Begin today. Challenge a negative thought, say 'no' when you mean it, or share an idea you've been holding back. With every small step, you reclaim your power and authenticity, discovering that the approval you truly need is your own.

CHAPTER 3

Creating a Personalized Self-Care Plan

> *"Caring for myself is not self-indulgence . . . it is self-preservation, and that is an act of political warfare."*
>
> *AUDRE LORDE*

Forsee the end of a long, chaotic day. The kind where every minute feels like it's been spoken for, meetings ran over, errands piled up, and your to-do list only seemed to grow. Finally, you sink into your favorite chair, the room dimly lit, a soft blanket draped across your lap. A gentle breeze wafts through an open window, carrying the scent of rain. As you close your eyes, the world outside fades, and for a moment, peace envelops you. This is self-care, not a luxury, but a necessity. It's an act of reclaiming yourself, of choosing to pause and tend to your mind, body, and spirit. Self-care isn't about indulgence or fleeting pleasures; it's about sustaining your well-being and replenishing your energy. It's the antidote to stress and the foundation for a healthy, balanced life.

Self-care is distinguished from indulgence by its intent and effect. While indulgence might offer temporary satisfaction, like zoning out with a pint of ice cream after a stressful day, self-care provides lasting benefits, such as journaling to process your emotions or taking a long walk to clear your mind. It's the difference between a quick escape and a meaningful recharge. Self-care reduces stress, enhances mental health, and fosters resilience. The grounding force equips you to face life's challenges with strength and clarity. By prioritizing self-care, you invest in your overall well-being, cultivating a life that thrives on balance and harmony. This practice is not a selfish act but an essential one, allowing you to be your best self in every role you play.

Identifying your self-care needs requires introspection and honesty. Begin by assessing your lifestyle and preferences. Deliberate on the emotional, physical, and social dimensions of your life. Emotionally, self-care might involve journaling, practicing gratitude, or setting boundaries in relationships. Physically, it could mean prioritizing sleep, engaging in gentle exercise, or nourishing your body with balanced meals. Socially, self-care might include calling a friend, joining a community group, or simply saying "no" to plans that drain your energy. Reflect on the moments when you feel most alive and at peace. Is it a quiet morning walk, a deep conversation with a friend, or time spent immersed in a creative pursuit? Understanding these needs is the first step in crafting a personalized self-care plan that honors who you are and what you need to flourish.

Self-awareness is crucial in effective self-care. It involves tuning into your body and mind, recognizing when you need rest and when you need stimulation. For instance, imagine you've had an exhausting week at work and feel on the verge of burnout. Through self-awareness, you might notice physical signs like tension in your shoulders or a racing mind at night. Emotionally, you might feel irritable or disconnected. By tuning into these signals, you can respond with empathy, perhaps by scheduling an early night, stepping away from screens for some quiet time, or reaching out to a friend for support. This practice fosters a deeper connection with yourself, enabling you to care for yourself more intuitively and effectively. By listening to your body and mind, you create a dialogue of compassion and care, reinforcing the importance of self-care in your daily life.

The nature of self-care is dynamic; it evolves as you do. For instance, during a particularly hectic work period, self-care might involve brief but focused practices like a five-minute breathing exercise or a quick walk around the block. In contrast, during a quieter season of life, you might embrace more immersive activities like a weekend getaway, a deep dive into a creative hobby, or attending a mindfulness retreat. By embracing the ebb and flow of your needs, you allow self-care to remain relevant and effective, offering solace and support through life's inevitable changes.

Interactive Element: Create Your Seasonal Self-Care Checklist

Self-care looks different depending on the time of year and the rhythm of your life. To help you stay refreshed and balanced, create a seasonal self-care checklist tailored to your unique needs and preferences. Start by brainstorming activities that bring you joy, peace, or energy for each season. Here are some examples to spark your ideas:

- **Spring:** Nature walks, gardening, journaling about new beginnings.
- **Summer:** Beach days, outdoor yoga, reading in the park.
- **Fall:** Cozy evenings with tea, reflective journaling, and craft projects.

• **Winter:** Warm baths, meditation, baking comfort foods.

Once you've created your checklist, revisit it at the start of each season and adjust as needed. This practice ensures your self-care routine stays aligned with your current needs, offering both variety and nourishment year-round.

Your self-care plan is like a garden; it thrives when nurtured consistently and adapted to the changing seasons. Begin today by taking a small step: reflect on one thing you need right now to feel more grounded and whole. Whether it's a moment of stillness, a conversation with someone you trust, or simply stepping outside for fresh air, honor that need. Remember, self-care isn't a luxury or an afterthought, it is an act of self-respect and love, the foundation for a life lived with intention and balance.

PART 1 DESIGNING YOUR ROUTINE: BALANCING MIND, BODY, AND SPIRIT

Creating a balanced self-care routine is like weaving a tapestry of well-being, where each thread represents the different facets of your life. To truly nurture yourself, it's important to address the needs of your mind, body, and spirit. This triadic model of self-care ensures that you're not just tending to one aspect of your being while neglecting others.

The mind, the center of your emotional and cognitive world, thrives on both stimulation and rest. Craft a vision of the satisfaction of solving a challenging puzzle or the serenity of a quiet meditation session. The body, your vessel for experiencing life, responds to your care with vitality and strength. Think of the grounding sensation of bare feet on grass during a nature walk or the release of tension after a deep stretch in yoga. The spirit, often neglected, is your inner compass, connected to your values and sense of purpose. Spiritual self-care might involve standing at the edge of the ocean, feeling the waves lap at your feet as you reconnect with something greater than yourself, or losing yourself in a creative project that makes your heart sing. Together, these elements create a harmony that nurtures your entire being.

To design a self-care routine that fits your life, start by reflecting on these questions:

- **Mind:** What activities stimulate or relax my mind?
- **Body:** How do I enjoy moving my body or caring for my physical health?
- **Spirit:** What brings me a sense of purpose, peace, or joy?

Write down a few activities for each category, and then think about how they might fit into your daily or weekly rhythms. For example, your daily self-care might include a five-minute morning gratitude practice to set a positive tone for the day, a brisk lunchtime walk to refresh your mind and body, and an evening journaling session to process your thoughts. Weekly, you might dedicate time for a creative hobby, like painting or backyard planting, or engage in a social activity that energizes you, such as meeting a friend for coffee or joining a group yoga class. By incorporating both short daily practices and longer weekly rituals, you create a rhythm of self-care that feels both manageable and fulfilling.

The benefits of holistic self-care extend far beyond the immediate sense of relaxation. For instance, integrating mindfulness practices like meditation or yoga can help you respond to stressful situations with greater calm and clarity. Creative expression might unlock new ideas or perspectives, sparking inspiration in your personal or professional life. Physical care, such as regular exercise or healthy eating, boosts your energy levels, allowing you to show up fully in your relationships and responsibilities. Over time, these practices build resilience, equipping you to navigate challenges with confidence and grace.

Flexibility is an important aspect of maintaining an effective self-care routine. Life is unpredictable, and trying to adhere rigidly to a set routine can sometimes add stress rather than alleviate it. Instead, view your routine as a living, breathing entity that can adapt to your current circumstances. For instance, if your morning starts earlier than usual due to a work meeting, you might shorten your meditation to three minutes or replace it with a moment of deep breathing on your commute. On days when you're feeling emotionally drained, you might skip a workout in favor of a restorative activity, like soaking in a warm bath or reading a favorite book. Flexibility ensures that self-care doesn't become another source of stress . . . it remains a tool for support and nourishment, meeting you exactly where you are.

Your self-care routine is not a rigid checklist. It's a dynamic and evolving guide designed to support you in every season of life. Start by weaving a single thread into your tapestry of well-being: commit to one small, meaningful act of self-care today, whether it's a few moments of reflection, a walk outside, or a creative endeavor that sparks joy. Over time, these small acts will grow into a routine that nourishes your mind, body, and spirit, helping you cultivate a life of balance, harmony, and resilience.

PART 2 PRACTICAL STEPS: IMPLEMENTING DAILY SELF-CARE PRACTICES

Incorporating self-care into your daily routine doesn't require a complete lifestyle overhaul. Instead, it's about making small, intentional changes that create a meaningful impact over time. Start with morning rituals that set a positive tone for the day. As you wake, resist the urge to reach for your phone. Instead, sit quietly for a moment, feeling the warmth of the sunlight filtering through your curtains. Take three deep breaths, each one an invitation to greet the day with calm and clarity. Perhaps you spend a few minutes journaling what you're grateful for or simply savor the rich aroma of your morning coffee as it warms your hands. These small rituals anchor your day in intention, offering a sense of control and optimism.

In the evening, establish wind-down routines that signal it's time to rest. Dim the lights and allow the busyness of the world to fade. Perhaps you curl up with a book, the rustle of pages creating a soothing rhythm, or you light a candle and let its soft glow center your thoughts. Listening to calming music or practicing gentle stretches can signal to your body that it's time to rest. These evening rituals are more than routines, they are invitations to let go of the day's stress and prepare your mind and body for rejuvenation.

Time management can be a major hurdle in prioritizing self-care, especially amidst busy schedules. To navigate this, envision time-blocking strategies that allocate specific periods for self-care activities. For example, if your afternoons often feel chaotic, block out 15 minutes between meetings to take a short walk or step away from your desk. Use your calendar to schedule a "self-care appointment," whether it's a quick yoga session at 6:30 p.m. or a Sunday morning reserved for journaling and reflection. Treat this time as non-negotiable, just as you would a work meeting or doctor's visit. Protect it by communicating your needs clearly to those around you. Let technology support your efforts by exploring self-care apps such as **Calm** or **Headspace** for guided meditations, **Habitica** to gamify habit tracking, or **Daylio** to track your mood and habits. These tools help you stay accountable and ensure that self-care remains a priority, even on the busiest days.

On particularly hectic days, micro self-care practices can be a life-saver. These are small, quick activities that fit seamlessly into your routine, providing a burst of refreshment and a pivotal point. For example:

- While commuting, listen to a favorite podcast or calming playlist to set a positive tone.
- At work, take 60 seconds to stretch your arms and shoulders or do a quick desk yoga pose to release tension.
- Between errands, pause to take five deep breaths, letting each exhale carry away stress.
- During meals, put your phone aside and savor each bite, noticing the textures and flavors.

These small acts may seem insignificant, but their cumulative effect can be profound, transforming scattered moments into opportunities for self-care and presence.

Consistency is key in building any habit, and self-care is no exception. Think of self-care as tending a rose garden. Each daily act of care, whether it's a moment of mindfulness, a nourishing meal, or a walk outside, is like watering a seed. At first, you may not see immediate results, but over time, your small, consistent efforts will help your roses flourish, yielding a life rich in health, balance, and fulfillment. To make self-care a habit, begin modestly and pair new practices with existing routines. For example, meditate right after brushing your teeth or practice gratitude as you brew your coffee. Track your progress with a self-care log, noting the activities you engage in and how they make you feel. Over time, this practice will reveal what works best for you and serve as a motivating reminder of your commitment to your well-being.

Start simply. Choose one self-care practice, a morning ritual, a micro-moment of mindfulness, or a weekly yoga session, and commit to it this week. Write it into your calendar, set a reminder on your phone, or pair it with an existing habit. Remember, self-care isn't about perfection or grand gestures, it's about showing up for yourself, one intentional act at a time. With each small step, you build a foundation of well-being that will support you in every aspect of your life.

PART 3 OVERCOMING GUILT: PRIORITIZING SELF WITHOUT SACRIFICE

It's an all-too-familiar feeling, the twinge of guilt that sneaks in when you pause to take a deep breath, sit down with a book, or even close your eyes for a moment of peace. That small voice whispers, *"Shouldn't you be doing something more productive?"* *"Shouldn't you be helping someone else?"* In a world that glorifies selflessness, taking time for yourself can feel like an indulgence you haven't earned. Society perpetuates the myth that to be virtuous is to give endlessly, often at the expense of your own well-being. This narrative convinces us that self-care is selfish, leaving many women battling guilt when they choose to prioritize their health and happiness. But the truth is this: self-care is not an indulgence, it's a lifeline. It's a practice that sustains not only your own well-being but also your ability to show up fully for the people and commitments that matter most.

Reframing self-care as a necessary practice rather than a guilty pleasure is a crucial step in overcoming this guilt. Start by viewing self-care as self-preservation, a vital act that sustains your ability to give and support others. It's about filling your cup so that you have the energy and resilience to navigate life's demands. For example, look at Anna, a working mother who rarely takes time for herself, believing every moment not spent working or parenting is selfish. One day, she decided to take a 30-minute walk each evening despite the guilt that crept in. To her surprise, this small act of self-care left her feeling calmer, more aligned, and more patient with her children. By reframing her walk as a way to recharge and show up more fully for her family, Anna shifted her perspective from guilt to gratitude.

To reinforce this mindset, reflect on adopting affirmations that promote self-acceptance and kindness. Repeat phrases like "I deserve care and compassion" or "Taking time for myself allows me to be my best." These affirmations help shift your perspective, reminding you that prioritizing your needs is an act of love, not selfishness.

Embracing self-compassion is another powerful tool in prioritizing self-care. Treat yourself with the same kindness and understanding you would offer a dear friend. When guilt arises, pause and ask yourself, *Would I judge a friend for taking a break or seeking comfort?* Chances are, the answer is no. Try this simple exercise to cultivate self-compassion: When guilt creeps in, recall a close friend feeling the same way. What would you say to reassure them? Write those words down and direct them to yourself. For example, you might say, "You're doing your best, and taking time for yourself is okay. Resting doesn't make you selfish; it makes you stronger." Practices like loving-kindness meditation can also help foster an empathetic inner dialogue.

Communicating your self-care needs to others is another vital step in alleviating guilt. For example, if you're feeling overwhelmed by family responsibilities, you might say to your partner, "I've been feeling stretched thin lately and realize I need some time to recharge. I'd like to take an hour each evening to go for a walk or read a book. Could we adjust our routine to make this happen?"

Or, if a friend invites you to an outing when you need rest, you might respond, "Thanks for thinking of me, but I need some downtime tonight to recharge. Let's plan something for next week instead." By clearly articulating your needs, you set the stage for healthier relationships that respect your well-being.

Setting boundaries is equally important. Use this framework to protect your self-care time:

1. **Identify Your Priorities:** Determine which self-care practices are most important to you and why.
2. **Choose Your Time:** Block off specific times for self-care on your calendar, whether it's 30 minutes in the morning or an hour on the weekend.
3. **Communicate Clearly:** Share your plans with those who might be affected. For example, say, "I've set aside Sunday mornings for yoga. Can we plan family activities around that time?"
4. **Enforce Gently:** If someone pushes against your boundaries, calmly reiterate them. For instance, "I understand you need my help, but I need to stick to this time for myself. Let's find another way to make it work."

By framing self-care as a priority and communicating it effectively, you model the importance of well-being, encouraging others to do the same.

Remember, prioritizing yourself isn't an act of selfishness, it's an act of courage and self-respect. This week, take one small step toward overcoming guilt. Maybe it's setting aside 10 minutes for yourself, practicing a self-compassion exercise, or having an open conversation about your needs with someone you trust. Each time you choose self-care, you're not just nurturing yourself, you're creating a ripple effect of balance and positivity in your relationships and beyond. Let go of the guilt, embrace your worth, and take that first step toward a more fulfilling, balanced life.

PART 4 THE ROLE OF MINDFULNESS: STAYING PRESENT IN SELF-CARE

Render the thought of yourself in the middle of a busy day: your mind racing with tasks, your shoulders tense, and your breath shallow. Now, let's pause for just a moment. You close your eyes, take a deep breath, and feel the air expand your chest before releasing it slowly. In that brief pause, the noise of the world quiets, and you reconnect with the present moment. This is mindfulness, a powerful practice that anchors you in the here and now. When woven into self-care, mindfulness transforms even the simplest activities into intentional acts of nurturing. Whether it's feeling the warmth of sunlight on your skin or savoring the aroma of your morning coffee, mindfulness invites you to be fully present, enhancing your well-being with every moment.

Incorporating mindfulness into your self-care practices can be as simple as introducing mindful movement into your exercise routine. Delve into a simple walk in the park. Rather than rushing to get steps in, slow down and center your thoughts on the sensations: the feel of your feet connecting with the ground, the rhythmic sway of your arms, and the sound of leaves rustling in the breeze. Notice your breath as it syncs with your movement, deepening with each step. This shift in awareness transforms a typical walk into a moving meditation, leaving you feeling grounded and refreshed. Similarly, during a yoga session, tune into the stretch of your muscles and the flow of your breath, allowing each pose to become an expression of mindfulness. These small adjustments elevate physical activity into a holistic practice that nourishes both body and mind.

Mindful listening is another way to bring presence into your self-care routine. Transport yourself sitting down with your favorite piece of music, not as background noise but as the centerpiece of your attention. Close your eyes and tune in to the layers of sound: the steady hum of a bassline, the delicate pluck of strings, or the soaring notes of a melody. Notice how the music makes you feel, does it evoke joy, nostalgia, or calm? This practice not only enhances your enjoyment but also deepens your connection to the present moment. The same approach applies to podcasts or audiobooks. Rather than multitasking, allow yourself to fully absorb the words, reflecting on the emotions and ideas they spark. By engaging your senses and emotions, mindful listening becomes a source of both pleasure and insight.

Mindful self-reflection offers an opportunity to tune into your inner world with greater clarity. After completing a self-care activity, whether it's a workout, a journaling session, or a quiet moment of meditation, sit quietly for a few minutes. Ask yourself reflective questions like:

- 'What sensations did I notice during this activity?'
- 'How do I feel emotionally and physically now?'
- 'What can I learn from this experience about my needs?'

Write your thoughts in a journal if it helps to process them further. For example, after a mindful walk, you might notice that the sound of birds or the rhythm of your steps brings you a sense of calm. These insights deepen your understanding of what nourishes you, helping you refine your self-care routine to better align with your evolving needs.

The benefits of mindfulness extend far beyond the moment of practice. For instance, by developing the ability to observe your emotions without judgment, you might find yourself responding to a frustrating situation with patience rather than anger. Regular mindfulness practice sharpens your lens, allowing you to approach work tasks with greater efficiency and creativity. Over time, these small shifts create a ripple effect, improving not only your sense of balance and well-being but also your relationships, productivity, and overall quality of life.

Begin your mindfulness journey today by choosing one simple practice. Whether it's a five-minute breathing exercise, a slow and intentional walk, or journaling your reflections after a self-care activity, commit to being fully present in that moment. Remember, mindfulness isn't about perfection, it's about curiosity and compassion. With each small act of mindfulness, you create space for peace, clarity, and connection to flourish in your life.

PART 5 INTERACTIVE JOURNALING: TRACKING YOUR SELF-CARE PROGRESS

Form a mental sketch each day as a fresh page in your life's story, waiting to be filled with moments of care, reflection, and discovery. As you pick up your pen and begin to write, the gentle scratch of ink on paper becomes a soothing rhythm, a conversation with yourself that reveals what nourishes your soul. Journaling is more than a record of your day; it's a sacred space to explore your thoughts, celebrate your victories, and confront your challenges honestly and gracefully. By keeping a self-care journal, you capture the small, significant moments that shape your well-being and create a map that guides you toward a more intentional and fulfilling life.

Incorporating prompts into your journaling practice can help guide your reflections and uncover meaningful insights. Speculate starting with questions like:

- "What self-care practice brought me the most joy today?"
- "What emotions surfaced during my self-care routine, and what might they be telling me?"
- "What's one small act of kindness I showed myself today, and how did it feel?"
- "What challenges arose today, and how can I support myself through them?"

These prompts not only help you track your progress but also encourage you to connect deeply with your emotions and experiences, fostering a greater sense of self-awareness.

If you're new to journaling, start with a simple three-step framework:

1. **Reflect:** Begin each entry by noting your current mood or energy level. Are you feeling calm, anxious, energized, or drained?
2. **Record:** Write about one self-care practice you engaged in that day. What did you do, and how did it make you feel?
3. **Refine:** Conclude with a question or intention for the next day. For example, "What can I do tomorrow to feel more balanced?"

This structure keeps your journaling centered while leaving room for creativity and exploration as you grow more comfortable with practice.

To keep journaling engaging and enjoyable, explore creative methods that resonate with your style and preferences. For those who love to express themselves visually, art journaling offers a therapeutic way to capture your thoughts and emotions. Pretend to fill your page with vibrant watercolors that reflect your mood, sketch symbols that represent your intentions, or paste magazine clippings to create a collage of inspiration. This approach turns your journal into a canvas for self-expression, where creativity and reflection intertwine.

Alternatively, bullet journaling may be your ideal method if you prefer structure and efficiency. Using simple lists, charts, or symbols, you can track your self-care activities, set goals, and monitor your progress over time. For instance, you might create a habit tracker to log daily practices like meditation, hydration, or exercise, offering a clear visual of your consistency. Both methods can be tailored to your preferences, ensuring your journaling practice feels personal and enjoyable.

Over time, journaling can reveal powerful insights. For instance, you might notice that taking a morning walk consistently energizes and optimizes you, prompting you to prioritize this practice. You might also discover that journaling about your emotions helps you process stress more effectively, allowing you to approach challenges more clearly and calmly. These small revelations can add up to meaningful changes, transforming your self-care routine into a source of strength and renewal.

Today, take a few minutes to open a blank page and let your thoughts flow. There's no right or wrong way to journal, only a commitment to showing up for yourself with curiosity and kindness. Whether you write a single sentence or fill an entire page, know that each word brings you closer to understanding yourself and your needs. Set the first stone, stay consistent, and watch as this practice transforms your self-care routine and your relationship with yourself. Your story is waiting, pick up the pen and begin.

CHAPTER 4

Setting Boundaries with Confidence

> "You have to teach people how to treat you by deciding what you will and won't accept."
>
> OPRAH WINFREY

I n your mind, see a lush and vibrant arboretum where each plant thrives in its own space. The roses stretch upward, their blooms kissed by the sunlight, while the ferns spread wide, their fronds swaying gently in the breeze. The gardener has carefully tended to each, ensuring roots have room to grow and branches have space to reach for the sky. Without these boundaries, without the right soil, sunlight, and care, plants would wither, overshadow each other, or become entangled, unable to thrive. Just like this grove of life, we need boundaries to create a flourishing life. These invisible lines define where we end and others begin, protecting the space we need to grow, rest, and blossom.

Boundaries come in many forms: physical, emotional, and mental. Physical boundaries are perhaps the easiest to visualize. For instance, you might feel uncomfortable when someone stands too close to you in a crowded room or hugs you without asking. Setting a physical boundary could mean stepping back, saying, "I prefer a little more space," or declining a hug with a kind but firm, "I'm not a hugger."

Emotional boundaries, on the other hand, involve protecting your emotional energy. Remember a friend venting to you about their problems for hours without asking how you're doing. Setting an emotional boundary might involve saying, "I care about you, but I need some time to recharge before we talk about this further."

Mental boundaries safeguard your thoughts and beliefs. For example, if someone constantly challenges your opinions in a way that feels dismissive, you might assert your mental boundary by saying, "I respect your perspective, but I'd appreciate it if we could have this discussion without dismissing my views." These examples show how boundaries empower you to protect your space, energy, and sense of self.

Without boundaries, life can quickly become overwhelming. Think about this: your boss asks you to stay late, even though you've already worked overtime all week. A friend calls, needing a favor, and you say yes, even though you're exhausted. Meanwhile, your family expects you to cook dinner despite your clear signals that you're stretched too thin. As you scramble to meet everyone else's needs, you realize you've skipped lunch, haven't had a moment to rest, and feel on the verge of burnout. Over time, this pattern erodes your sense of self, leaving you drained, resentful, and disconnected from your own needs. This is the cost of weak boundaries, and it's why setting and maintaining them is essential.

Interactive Element: Boundary Assessment Exercise

Take a moment to reflect on your current boundaries. Use the following prompts to guide your thoughts:

1. **Identify Stress Points:**
   - In which areas of your life do you feel most overwhelmed?
   - Are there specific situations or people that consistently leave you feeling drained?
2. **Examine Your Responses:**
   - When was the last time you said yes to something you didn't want to do?
   - Do you feel guilty when you prioritize your needs? Why?
3. **Set One New Boundary:**
   - Think of one area where you need more space or balance. What small action can you take this week to reinforce that boundary? For example, you could:
     - Say no to an extra commitment.
     - Block off 30 minutes for yourself on your calendar.
     - Politely decline a request that feels overwhelming.

Write down your answers and revisit them at the end of the week to reflect on how setting that boundary impacted your energy and well-being.

This week, give yourself permission to protect your vigor and vitality. Start with baby steps, say no to one thing that doesn't serve you, or set aside time for yourself without guilt. Remember, boundaries are not walls but bridges to a more balanced, fulfilling life. By setting clear limits, you create space for what truly matters:

your growth, your peace, and your joy. Take the first step today and watch as your green oasis begins to thrive.

PART 1 COMMUNICATING BOUNDARIES: ASSERTIVENESS WITHOUT AGGRESSION

Visualize standing in a crowded room, your voice steady as you express your needs with clarity and confidence. Perhaps it's a meeting where you feel overwhelmed by additional responsibilities or a conversation with a friend who's been leaning heavily on your emotional support. In these moments, the ability to communicate your boundaries assertively can make all the difference. Assertive communication is the art of expressing your needs clearly and confidently without aggression or passivity. It's about saying, "This is what I need," while remaining open to dialogue and compromise. Unlike aggression, which seeks to dominate, assertiveness is rooted in mutual respect and clarity, a skill that fosters understanding rather than conflict.

Articulating boundaries clearly can sometimes feel daunting, but there are techniques that make it manageable. Using "I" statements shifts the emphasis to your own feelings and needs, avoiding language that might come across as accusatory. For instance, instead of saying, "You always interrupt me," which could feel confrontational, you might say, "I feel unheard when I'm interrupted, and I'd appreciate a chance to finish my thoughts." This approach minimizes defensiveness and opens the door for productive dialogue.

Setting clear limits also reinforces your boundaries while maintaining respect for others. For example, saying, "I can help for an hour, but then I need to leave," signals your willingness to assist without overextending yourself. These techniques create clarity and prevent misunderstandings, ensuring that your needs are communicated effectively.

Balancing assertiveness with empathy strengthens your ability to maintain boundaries while fostering connection. Recall a friend who frequently calls to vent about their problems. You might feel torn between wanting to support them and needing space for your own well-being. An empathetic yet assertive response could sound like, "I hear how difficult this is for you, and I want to be there for you. But I've been feeling overwhelmed and need some time to recharge. Can we talk again tomorrow when I'm in a better place to listen?" This response validates their feelings while clearly communicating your limits.

Active listening is a key component of this balance. It involves not just hearing but reflecting the other person's perspective back to them. For example, saying, "It sounds like you're feeling stressed about this project, and I can understand why," shows that you're engaged in the conversation. When paired with a clear boundary, like, "I'd love to help brainstorm solutions, but I can only do so for 30 minutes today," this approach fosters mutual respect and understanding.

Gauge this scenario of negotiating work-life balance with a manager. You may feel overwhelmed by an increasing workload but hesitant to speak up for fear of seeming uncommitted. Using assertive communication, you might say, "I truly value the opportunity to work on this project, and I want to ensure I give it my best. To do that, I need to balance my time more effectively. Can we review the deadlines and prioritize the most critical tasks?" This approach shows respect for your manager's goals while advocating for your own needs, paving the way for a constructive and collaborative conversation.

As you begin to practice assertive communication, remember that it's a skill that takes time and patience to develop. Concentrate on the first part of the plan, perhaps with a simple "I" statement in a conversation with a reliable partner or setting a limit on your time at work. Each time you assert your needs with clarity and respect, you move deliberately toward stronger boundaries and healthier relationships. Your voice matters, and by using it with confidence and empathy, you create a life where your needs are heard, understood, and respected.

PART 2 ROLE-PLAYING SCENARIOS: PRACTICING BOUNDARY SETTING

Conjure in your mind as you step into a scene where you can safely experiment with setting boundaries, no judgment, just exploration. In this scene, there is a quiet room, a beloved friend sitting across from you, and the air is filled with a sense of collaboration and possibility. You take a deep breath, steadying your voice as you practice articulating your needs. This is the beauty of role-playing: a space to rehearse life's essential conversations without the pressure of real-world consequences. Here, you can try out different phrases, adjust your tone, and explore what feels most authentic. It's like a dress rehearsal for setting boundaries, allowing you to build confidence, refine your approach, and step into real-life situations feeling prepared and empowered.

Ponder a scenario where your manager asks you to take on an additional project at work. You already feel stretched thin, and the thought of more responsibility is overwhelming. In a role-play, you might practice saying, "I appreciate the opportunity, but my current workload is at capacity. I want to ensure I deliver my best on existing projects." As you rehearse, notice how it feels to express your limits, perhaps a mix of relief and nerves. This practice not only helps you find the right words but also allows you to process the emotions that come with setting professional boundaries.

Now, here is a thoughtful storyboard, a family gathering, where an opinionated relative begins offering unsolicited advice about your life. Their words feel invasive, and you feel a familiar tension rising in your chest. In a role-play, you might practice responding with, "Thank you for your input, but I need to make this decision on my own." By rehearsing this response, you can experiment with tones that convey respect while firmly asserting your autonomy. This scenario helps you navigate the delicate balance between maintaining family harmony and upholding your personal boundaries.

Digital boundaries are becoming increasingly relevant in a world of constant connectivity. And here comes your friend who expects immediate responses to their texts, and you feel guilty every time you don't reply right away. In a role-play, you might rehearse saying, "I value our friendship and love chatting with you, but I'm trying to spend less time on my phone for my mental health. Can we set up a weekly catch-up instead?" Practicing this allows you to articulate your needs around digital communication without feeling dismissive, reinforcing your boundaries while showing care for the relationship.

How to Structure a Role-Playing Session

1. **Choose a Scenario:** Identify a boundary-setting situation that feels challenging for you, such as saying no to extra work or addressing a friend's overstepping behavior.
2. **Set the Scene:** Describe the context to your role-play partner. For example, "You're my manager, and you've just asked me to stay late again this week."

3. **Practice Your Lines:** Use "I" statements and clear, respectful language to articulate your needs. Don't worry if it feels awkward at first, this is your space to experiment.

4. **Reflect and Adjust:** After the role-play, ask your partner for feedback and reflect on what felt natural and what could be improved. Try the scenario again, incorporating what you've learned.

5. **Repeat and Reinforce:** Practice multiple scenarios to build a repertoire of responses, strengthening your confidence and adaptability.

Remember, role-playing isn't about getting it perfect . . . it's about giving yourself the freedom to explore, experiment, and grow. Begin with a tiny seed, perhaps with a faithful friend, or even by practicing alone in front of a mirror. With each session, you'll find yourself becoming more comfortable and confident in asserting your needs. Boundary-setting is a skill; like any skill, it gets easier with practice. Step into your role-playing rehearsal today and watch your ability to communicate boundaries transform.

PART 3 REAL-LIFE SUCCESS STORIES: EMPOWERMENT THROUGH BOUNDARIES

In the world of professional chaos, Mitzi's life was a whirlwind of back-to-back meetings, overflowing emails, and endless to-do lists. Her career as a project manager was thriving, but her personal life felt like it was crumbling. She described her days as a treadmill that never stopped, exhausting, relentless, and isolating. Once her time to unwind, evenings were swallowed by work, leaving her drained and disconnected from herself and her loved ones. One evening, as she stared at her laptop long after sunset, she decided enough was enough.

Mitzi began setting clear boundaries: no more emails after 6 PM, lunch breaks were non-negotiable, and weekends became sacred personal time. At first, the shift felt unnatural, even defiant, as if she were breaking an unwritten rule of professional sacrifice. But as the weeks went by, her life began to change. Her evenings turned into a sanctuary of stillness, filled with music, books, and moments of creativity. Weekends became a canvas for joy, laughter-filled dinners with friends, walks in the park, and the simple bliss of doing nothing. By holding firm to her boundaries, Mitzi reclaimed her time and energy, rediscovering the balance and fulfillment she thought she had lost. Her story is a testament to the power of boundaries, showing how a few intentional changes can transform both personal and professional lives.

Marletta was a mother whose days were consumed by the endless demands of family life. From the moment her alarm rang to the last dish washed at night, her time belonged to everyone but herself. Caring for her children, managing household tasks, and juggling countless responsibilities left her feeling invisible, her own identity buried under the weight of her obligations. She was exhausted, frustrated, and deeply aware that something needed to change.

One day, she decided to take a bold step: to set boundaries that prioritized her well-being. At first, it felt selfish, even impossible, but she reminded herself that self-care wasn't an indulgence; it was survival. She began carving out small pockets of time each day, starting with a quiet hour in the morning for yoga and reflection. After tucking her children into bed in the evenings, she claimed an hour just for herself, diving into novels that transported her to another world. These moments became her lifeline.

Communicating her needs to her family was challenging at first. "I love you all," she told them, "But I need some time each day to recharge so I can show up for you fully." The transformation was remarkable. Marletta found herself more patient, more present, and more joyful with her family. Her boundaries didn't just restore her sense of self; they brought new depth to her relationships, showing her loved ones that taking care of herself ultimately allowed her to give more freely to them.

PART 4 OVERCOMING BOUNDARY GUILT: PUTTING YOURSELF FIRST

You're asked to help with yet another project at work, even though your schedule is already packed. Or perhaps a family member asks for a favor, and you feel that familiar twinge of guilt at the thought of saying no. Many of us have been conditioned to believe that prioritizing others is a sign of virtue and that selflessness equals worthiness. But this mindset often comes at a cost: the quiet erosion of our energy, well-being, and even our sense of self.

Setting boundaries can feel radical, even uncomfortable, because it challenges these deeply ingrained beliefs. Saying no or putting yourself first might stir feelings of guilt, a voice in your head whispering, "You're being selfish." But here's the paradox: by constantly putting others first, you risk depleting your own energy, leaving little for yourself or those you care about. Reframing boundaries as acts of self-care and even kindness can help you release this guilt and embrace the freedom that comes with honoring your needs.

Reframing boundaries as acts of kindness, both to yourself and others, can help ease feelings of guilt. Setting clear boundaries prevents misunderstandings and resentment, ensuring healthier, more sustainable relationships. It's like saying, "This is how I can best support you while also caring for myself." Create these boundaries as a protective shield that allows you to engage with others without losing yourself. Visualizing how setting a boundary today creates space for more meaningful connections tomorrow. To reinforce this mindset, try affirmations like, "I am worthy of care and respect." or "My needs are important." These simple yet powerful reminders can help counteract guilt and affirm your right to prioritize yourself.

Self-compassion is a cornerstone of overcoming boundary guilt. Treat yourself with the same kindness and understanding you'd extend to a dear friend. For instance, if you feel guilty about declining a last-minute social invitation, pause and ask yourself, "Would I judge a friend for saying no to protect their energy?" Likely, the answer is no.

Try this exercise: write a letter to yourself as if you were a friend, offering encouragement and understanding about your decision to set a boundary. For example: "I know it's hard to say no, but you're doing this because you deserve rest and respect. Setting this boundary doesn't make you selfish, it makes you strong." Writing these words can help shift your inner dialogue, replacing guilt with self-acceptance.

The impact of guilt-free boundaries on your well-being is profound. Imagine waking up without the weight of constant obligation on your shoulders, knowing that your time and energy are being spent intentionally. When you release the guilt tied to saying no, you make room for authentic interactions, conversations that feel lighter, freer, and more honest. Stress diminishes, and burnout fades as you reclaim control over your life.

Relationships flourish in this clarity. Instead of unspoken expectations and hidden resentments, you engage openly and authentically, fostering mutual respect and understanding. For example, a friend who once leaned too heavily on your emotional energy now understands and values your limits, deepening your bond. Even more, you begin to model healthy behavior for those around you, inspiring them to set boundaries of their own. This ripple effect creates a world where self-care is normalized and celebrated.

Releasing guilt isn't just about setting boundaries, it's about reclaiming your right to live authentically and joyfully. When you honor your needs, you empower yourself to show up fully for the people and passions that matter most. Start small: identify one area of your life where guilt is holding you back from setting a boundary. Practice reframing that boundary as an act of kindness and self-care, not selfishness. With each step, you'll find that the guilt fades, replaced by a deep sense of strength and self-respect. Remember, boundaries aren't walls; they're bridges to healthier relationships, greater peace, and a life where you can thrive.

PART 5 BUILDING RESILIENCE: HANDLING BOUNDARY PUSHBACK

So, you've just told your family that weekends are now dedicated to personal time, but your sibling responds with an exaggerated sigh and says, "After everything I've done for you, you can't even spare a few hours?" Or how about explaining to a coworker that you won't be checking emails after 6 PM, only for them to reply, "Wow, must be nice to just clock out like that." These moments of resistance can feel like subtle daggers, stirring guilt and doubt, making you question whether your boundaries were too harsh or unnecessary.

But here's the truth: pushback is often not about you, it's about others grappling with change. When you set boundaries, you disrupt the status quo, and that discomfort can lead to resistance.

The key is to remember that your boundaries are a reflection of your needs, not a reflection of your worth.

Remaining firm and consistent is key to handling resistance. Calmly repeating your needs reinforces your stance while showing others that your boundaries are not negotiable. For instance, if a family member insists on revisiting a sensitive topic, you might say, "I appreciate your concern, but I'm not comfortable discussing this right now." Restating your boundaries with kindness but firmness sends a clear message that you value your limits.

Similarly, seeking support from allies, friends, mentors, or even therapists can provide much-needed encouragement. They can offer perspective, reinforce your confidence, or even help mediate tough situations. Having someone remind you of the importance of your boundaries can make a world of difference when faced with pushback.

Building resilience in the face of resistance is an ongoing practice. Visualization exercises can be particularly effective in strengthening your resolve. When you find yourself in situations where your boundaries are respected and upheld, imagine the positive outcomes that follow. This mental rehearsal can boost your confidence, preparing you for real-life interactions. Stress management techniques, like deep breathing exercises, can also help you maintain composure during challenging exchanges. By cultivating these practices, you increase your capacity to handle resistance with grace and poise, transforming potential confrontations into opportunities for growth and understanding.

Jordan's demanding boss had become the center of her stress. She often stayed late, answering last-minute emails or picking up extra tasks with no warning. It left her drained, her evenings a blur of exhaustion, and her weekends spent recovering instead of living.

One day, as Jordan stared at yet another email marked "urgent," she realized she couldn't keep going this way. Summoning courage, she began setting boundaries. She told her boss, "I'm happy to contribute during work hours, but I'm not available after 6 PM." At first, the resistance was palpable. Her boss sighed loudly in meetings, piling on extra tasks to test her resolve. But Jordan remained consistent. She stuck to her schedule, turned off notifications in the evening, and refused to waver. Slowly, her boss began to adjust, redirecting urgent tasks earlier in the day and respecting her availability.

The result? Jordan rediscovered balance. Evenings became hers again, filled with dinner with friends, exercise, and much-needed rest. Her productivity at work improved, and her boss even began complimenting her ability to manage her workload efficiently. Jordan's story shows that even in challenging environments, resilience and consistency can create change.

Annette felt tethered to her phone, a constant stream of messages and notifications demanding her attention. Her friends expected immediate replies, and any delay was met with, "Are you okay?" or "Why are you ignoring me?" The pressure to always be available left her frazzled and overwhelmed.

One evening, after realizing she hadn't gone an hour without checking her phone, Annette decided to set digital boundaries. She messaged her closest friends, saying, "I'm trying to limit my screen time, so I'll only be checking messages in the morning and evening. Thanks for understanding!" At first, some friends resisted, sending sarcastic comments like, "Must be nice to ignore everyone!" or double-texting to get her attention. But Annette held fast. She ignored non-urgent messages during the day and turned off notifications while she worked.

Over time, her friends adjusted. Some even admired her discipline and began setting boundaries of their own. Annette found that when she did respond, her conversations felt more intentional and connected. Her digital detox didn't just improve her relationships, it brought a sense of calm and clarity to her entire day.

As we conclude this chapter, remember that pushback is not a reflection of your worth but of others' discomfort with change. Setting boundaries is an act of self-respect and courage. Each time you uphold your limits, you strengthen your ability to live authentically and confidently.

Reflect on a situation where you've faced resistance to a boundary. What strategies could you use to remain firm? Visualize how standing your ground can lead to a healthier dynamic and a more balanced life. Pushback is inevitable, but with resilience, consistency, and support, you have the power to protect your space and thrive. Take that first step, your well-being is worth it.

A Note of Gratitude and an Invitation to Share

Thank you for allowing this book to be a part of your journey. It has been my hope that the words within these pages have inspired you, challenged you, and reminded you of your own incredible power to grow, transform, and shine. As you close this chapter and continue crafting the life you deserve, I'd like to ask one final favor: if this book has touched your heart, sparked a meaningful change, or offered you tools to thrive, would you consider sharing your experience with others?

Your voice has the power to inspire someone else who might be standing where you once were—unsure, searching, and ready for a sign. By leaving a review on Amazon, you can help this message reach those who need it most. Your thoughts don't just reflect your journey; they create ripples of encouragement, helping others take that first brave step toward a more empowered life.

PAY IT FORWARD

If you feel compelled, I'd love to hear how this book has impacted your life. Did it give you a tool you needed, a perspective that shifted, or an affirmation that lifted your spirit? By sharing your story, you light the way for someone else to begin theirs.

As a small token of inspiration, let me leave you with this thought:

> *"The meaning of life is to find your gift. The purpose of life is to give it away."*

PABLO PICASSO

Your review is a gift—one that could inspire others to uncover their own strength, find clarity in their struggles, or take a leap they've been too afraid to make.

Thank you for paying it forward what you've learned and for being part of this shared journey of growth and empowerment. Your words, just like your actions, have the power to create meaningful change.

With gratitude and admiration,

Zara Imani

For Review Link Click Hereor use this QR Code!

CHAPTER 5

Building a Supportive Community

> *"What you do makes a difference, and you have to decide what kind of difference you want to make."*
>
> JANE GOODALL

Here, you find yourself at a crossroads, unsure of your next step. As you pause, a group of women gathers around you. They don't tell you which path to take, but their presence fills you with strength and confidence. You feel less alone, more assured, ready to move forward.

This image captures the essence of community, a network of individuals who walk alongside you, providing the support and encouragement you need to navigate life's complexities. For example, study a woman starting a new chapter in her career. Overwhelmed by doubt, she joins a professional network and meets a mentor who helps her see her potential. Or perhaps a new mother who joins a parenting group and finds solace in shared stories and advice. These moments of connection are what make communities so vital, offering the emotional, practical, and moral support we all need to thrive.

The importance of community cannot be overstated. Within a supportive network, you find a safe space to share your vulnerabilities and triumphs without fear of judgment. This emotional support fosters a sense of belonging and strengthens your connection to others, reducing feelings of isolation and loneliness. Communities also provide moral encouragement, reflecting back the potential and worth you might struggle to see in yourself. The voices of those who believe in you can act as a guiding light during times of doubt, helping you face challenges with greater confidence. Beyond emotional support, communities offer practical benefits like collaborative problem-solving and shared resources. When challenges arise, brainstorming with a group often leads to innovative solutions, transforming individual struggles into shared victories. Together, these benefits create a tapestry of support where personal growth flourishes through collective strength.

Communities come in many forms, each offering unique opportunities for connection and growth. Local groups, such as book clubs or gardening collectives, provide spaces to share interests and foster friendships. These informal gatherings often create deep bonds through shared passions. Professional networks, like industry associations or peer mentoring circles, open doors for career advancement and skill-building while connecting you with like-minded individuals who share your ambitions. Digital communities, whether online forums, social media groups, or virtual meetups, are equally valuable, providing connection when in-person interaction isn't possible. By exploring a variety of communities, you create a diverse support system that addresses different aspects of your life and interests.

Building a community that resonates with your values and interests begins with small, intentional steps. Start by identifying areas of your life where connection feels most needed, whether it's personal, professional, or creative. From there, take one actionable step this week. Attend a local meetup, join an online group, or simply reach out to an old friend to reconnect. Remember, community isn't built overnight, it grows through consistent effort and shared experiences.

Use the following checklist to guide your journey:

- **Attend a local meetup:** Find groups that align with your interests, such as writing workshops or hiking clubs.
- **Volunteer regularly:** Choose a cause you care about and commit to supporting it consistently.
- **Host a gathering:** Invite friends or acquaintances to a casual event, fostering connections in a relaxed setting.
- **Join a professional network:** Participate in industry-related events or online forums to connect with peers.

Each of these steps is an opportunity to create bonds that support and inspire you. As you engage with your community, remember that the connections you build not only enrich your own life but also empower those around you. Together, you create a network of strength, resilience, and belonging.

PART 1 FINDING YOUR TRIBE: BUILDING A NETWORK OF SUPPORT

Think about a moment when you felt truly understood, when someone shared your enthusiasm, supported your dreams, or simply listened with genuine care. Now, factor in walking into a room filled with people who offer that same sense of connection and understanding. This is the magic of finding your tribe, a group of like-minded individuals who not only share your values and goals but also inspire and uplift you as you journey through life.

The journey to finding your tribe begins with stepping into spaces where your interests thrive. Attend meetups fixated on your passions, whether it's a writing workshop, a yoga class, or a tech seminar. Clara, for example, discovered her tribe when she joined a local writing group. What started as a weekly meeting turned into a close-knit community that exchanged feedback, shared ideas, and celebrated each other's successes. Similarly, Jason, a tech enthusiast, found his tribe at a coding seminar, where he connected with peers who now collaborate with him on creative projects. These gatherings provide fertile ground for meeting people who resonate with your pursuits and values.

Your existing social circles can also be a treasure trove of untapped connections. Engage in deeper conversations with acquaintances or friends to uncover shared interests and values. Sometimes, the seeds of your tribe are already planted, waiting for the right moment to bloom. Community events like workshops, volunteer projects, or cultural gatherings are also excellent opportunities to expand your network and discover people who inspire and support you.

A supportive tribe is built on mutual respect and understanding. It's about creating a space where everyone feels valued and heard, and where differences are embraced rather than judged. Within such a network, encouragement flows freely, lifting each member higher. Accountability also plays a crucial role. When your tribe holds you accountable, checking in on your progress and celebrating your wins, it becomes easier to stay on track. This environment nurtures growth and fosters a sense of belonging, creating a haven where you can flourish.

Building meaningful relationships within your tribe requires active listening and empathy. When you engage with others, truly listen to their stories and perspectives. This practice not only deepens your connection but also enriches your understanding of the world through their experiences. Consistent communication and regular check-ins, whether it's a weekly coffee date or a thoughtful text, help maintain and strengthen these bonds over time.

Vulnerability is the key that unlocks deep, meaningful connections. By sharing your struggles, fears, and triumphs, you create a space for trust and authenticity. Initially, begin by asking for some advice or sharing how you've been feeling lately. These moments of openness invite others to do the same, strengthening the bonds of your tribe. Equally important is expressing your needs and boundaries clearly. Transparency sets the tone for healthy interactions, ensuring that your relationships are built on understanding and mutual respect.

Interactive Element: Connection Map Exercise

Create a connection map to visualize your current network and identify areas for growth:

- **Step 1:** Write your name in the center of a blank page. Around it, list the people you feel connected to, drawing lines to represent your relationships.
- **Step 2:** Use different colors or symbols to indicate the strength of each connection (e.g., a bold line for strong relationships, a dashed line for ones you'd like to strengthen).

- **Step 3:** Reflect on your map:
  - Which relationships bring you the most joy and support?
  - Are there connections you'd like to nurture further?
  - Where might you seek new relationships to fill gaps in your network?
- **Step 4:** Choose one action you can take this week to strengthen or build a connection.

Whether it's sending a thoughtful message, scheduling a coffee date, or attending a new event, these small steps can help you grow a more robust and supportive tribe.

Finding your tribe is a journey, but with each meaningful connection you make, you create a network that uplifts, supports, and empowers you to thrive.

PART 2 DIGITAL CONNECTIONS: LEVERAGING ONLINE COMMUNITIES

Suppose finding a group of people who share your passions, inspire your growth, and offer unwavering support, all with just a few clicks. In today's interconnected world, the digital landscape has made this possible. Whether it's joining a vibrant forum of like-minded individuals or connecting with an inspiring Instagram community, online platforms open doors to connections that transcend borders. These virtual spaces are more than just meeting places; they're lifelines of encouragement, creativity, and belonging in a fast-paced world.

Online platforms offer unparalleled opportunities to connect with people across the globe. Virtual support groups, like forums and Facebook groups, provide spaces for individuals to share experiences, exchange advice, and offer encouragement. Many of these groups are topic-specific, allowing participants to dive into discussions that matter most to them, whether it's mental health, creative hobbies, or career development. Social media platforms like Instagram and LinkedIn take these connections even further, enabling real-time conversations and collaborations. The beauty of these communities lies in their accessibility; you can engage from the comfort of your home, breaking down geographical barriers and finding a sense of belonging in a digital world.

The key to navigating this vast landscape is discernment. Before diving into a group, take time to research and vet communities carefully. Look for spaces that align with your values and goals, and review their guidelines to ensure a supportive and welcoming environment. For example, Sarah, a recent college graduate navigating her first job, joined a LinkedIn group for young professionals. Through this network, she found not only career advice but also mentors who helped her grow. Similarly, Jamal, an amateur photographer, connected with a supportive Instagram community that shared tips and constructive feedback on his work. These examples show how aligning with the right community can create meaningful and transformative connections.

While digital communities provide flexibility and reach, they also come with unique challenges. The lack of face-to-face interaction can sometimes hinder the development of deeper relationships, and the vastness of the internet means that misinformation can spread easily. To ensure a positive experience, approach online content critically, being mindful of the sources you trust and the information you share. Balancing online and offline interactions is equally important. While digital connections can be enriching, in-person relationships provide the warmth and depth that online interactions sometimes lack. Make time for face-to-face interactions, whether through coffee meetups, hobby groups, or professional networking events, to create a harmonious balance.

To make the most of your online interactions, adopt best practices that foster meaningful relationships. Participate regularly in discussions to build rapport with other members and stay engaged with the community. Share your insights, offer constructive feedback, and express genuine interest in others' experiences. These practices not only strengthen your connections but also enrich the community as a whole. At the same time, prioritize quality over quantity; it's better to be deeply involved in a few meaningful communities than to spread yourself too thin across many.

Balancing Digital and Offline Connections

While online communities provide incredible flexibility, they should complement, not replace, your offline relationships. Schedule regular activities that align with your digital interests. For instance, if you're part of an online book club, speculate on organizing an in-person meetup with local members. If you've connected with a professional network online, look for opportunities to attend industry events or conferences. By integrating your online and offline connections, you ensure that your social life remains dynamic, balanced, and fulfilling.

The digital world offers endless opportunities to build connections that inspire and uplift you. Start today by exploring communities that align with your passions and goals. Look for a group, forum, or social media community that resonates with you, and take the first step by introducing yourself or sharing your story. Remember, building meaningful relationships takes time and effort, but each interaction brings you closer to a network that enriches your life. By blending digital and in-person connections, you can create a support system that empowers you to thrive.

PART 3 TESTIMONIALS: THE POWER OF SHARED EXPERIENCES

Maggie had spent ten years building a career she thought would last a lifetime. When she unexpectedly lost her job, the stability she'd always relied on seemed to vanish overnight. Her days became filled with self-doubt and sleepless nights, haunted by questions like, "What now?" and "Am I enough?" In the midst of this uncertainty, Maggie came across a local support group for professionals in transition. Unsure of what to expect, she hesitated before deciding to attend her first meeting. What she found there surprised her: a room full of understanding faces, people who nodded as she spoke, offering words of encouragement from their own experiences. Over time, the group became a lifeline, providing not just emotional support but also practical advice. With their help, Maggie secured a new job and discovered a renewed sense of purpose, proving to herself that setbacks can pave the way for growth.

Lynnette had always dreamed of bringing her creative vision to life, but as a budding entrepreneur, she often felt alone in her efforts. Her apartment became her workspace, scattered with unfinished plans and endless to-do lists. Overwhelmed and unsure of how to move forward, she joined a collaborative workspace that promised more than just a desk. There, she met graphic designers, marketers, and other creative professionals who shared her passion for innovation. Through countless brainstorming sessions over coffee and late nights spent planning, Lynnette found not only the tools and expertise she needed but also partners who believed in her vision. Together, they tackled challenges that once felt insurmountable, launching her dream business to success. Her story is a testament to the transformative power of collaboration, showing how the strength of a community can turn aspirations into reality.

What makes these stories resonate so deeply is their ability to foster connection and inspire change. When someone shares their journey, whether it's overcoming a loss, pursuing a dream, or navigating uncertainty, they create a bridge of understanding. For instance, someone grappling with self-doubt might hear Maggie's story and realize they're not alone in their fears. Likewise, an aspiring entrepreneur might find courage in Lynnette's journey, knowing that collaboration and perseverance can lead to success. The authenticity in these stories, sharing not just triumphs but also vulnerabilities, allows others to see reflections of their own struggles and feel less isolated. It's this raw honesty that turns testimonials into beacons of hope and encouragement.

Sharing your own story can feel daunting, but it's also incredibly empowering. Start by reflecting on moments in your life when you overcame challenges or discovered strength you didn't know you had. Ask yourself:

- "What was my biggest struggle, and how did I grow from it?"
- "Who supported me along the way, and what did I learn from them?"
- "What message do I want others to take away from my journey?"

Create clarity on sharing your story through platforms like community blogs, newsletters, or even local support groups. These spaces allow you to reach people who might be facing similar challenges, offering them guidance and inspiration. As you give voice to your experiences, you may find that the act of sharing is not just cathartic but also deeply meaningful, creating connections that ripple far beyond your own circle.

The beauty of shared stories lies in their ripple effect. When Maggie shared her fears and triumphs, she not only found solace but also inspired others in her group to open up about their own journeys. When Lynnette collaborated with her community, their shared successes echoed through their networks, encouraging others to believe in the power of teamwork. Each story creates a spark, illuminating the paths of those who hear it. Together, these narratives weave a tapestry of resilience and hope, reminding us that we are all connected by our struggles, our growth, and our ability to lift one another. By sharing your own story, you become a thread in this tapestry, contributing to a collective strength that inspires and empowers us all.

PART 4 MENTORSHIP AND SUPPORT: LEARNING FROM OTHERS

Project this thought: you're sitting across from someone who has not only faced the challenges you're navigating but has also emerged stronger, wiser, and ready to share their journey. They don't just give you advice, they listen, empathize, and offer insights that make you feel seen and capable of achieving your dreams. This is the power of mentorship: a relationship that goes beyond guidance, offering a lifeline of wisdom, support, and inspiration. In the presence of a mentor, you gain not only knowledge but also the confidence to overcome obstacles, knowing someone believes in your potential.

Mentors provide a wealth of knowledge drawn from their own experiences, offering not just answers but the right questions to guide your growth. They serve as a beacon, illuminating the path to personal and professional development. The benefits of mentorship are profound. A mentor can open doors to opportunities you may not have considered, providing insights that challenge your perspectives and push you beyond your current horizon. In their stories and advice, you find the motivation to persevere, knowing someone believes in your capacity to achieve great things.

Take the story of Priya, a young professional stepping into her first leadership role. Overwhelmed by the demands of managing a team, she sought out a mentor, her company's HR director, whose calm and effective leadership style she admired. Through regular conversations, her mentor shared practical strategies for building trust with her team while managing her own workload. Priya didn't just gain tools for success; she also found reassurance in hearing her mentor's struggles from years ago. These insights gave her the confidence to lead with authenticity and balance.

Finding the right mentor begins with clarity. Reflect on your goals and ask yourself: "What do I hope to learn or achieve with guidance?" Once you've identified your needs, take these steps:

1. **Leverage Professional Networks:** Platforms like LinkedIn or local industry events are fertile ground for connecting with potential mentors. Look for individuals whose careers or values align with your aspirations.
2. **Reach Out Thoughtfully:** Send a personalized message or introduce yourself in person, expressing your admiration for their work and your desire to learn from them. Be specific about why you're reaching out and how you envision the mentorship relationship.
3. **Cultivate Informal Mentorships:** Not all mentors are found through formal programs.

Seek advice from colleagues, community members, or even family friends whose experiences resonate with you. Sometimes, mentorship emerges organically through ongoing conversations and shared interests.

Mentorship thrives on mutual respect and open communication. As a mentee, approach the relationship with humility and curiosity, being open to feedback and committed to applying your mentor's guidance. At the same time, respect your mentor's time and effort, demonstrating your gratitude through action. The most successful mentorships are dynamic exchanges, where both mentor and mentee grow and learn together.

As you benefit from mentorship, debate stepping into the mentor role yourself. Sharing your knowledge and experiences with others not only aids their development but enriches your own. Teaching often brings clarity to your own journey, deepening your understanding of your experiences. Mentorship also builds a sense of purpose, as you contribute to the growth of others and strengthen your community. By becoming a mentor, you continue a tradition of shared wisdom and empowerment, proving that growth is not a solitary pursuit but a collective endeavor.

Whether you're seeking guidance or ready to share your wisdom, mentorship has the power to transform lives, yours included. Take the first step today: reach out to someone whose journey inspires you, or offer your insights to someone navigating a path you've walked before. What about the ripple effect you could create, a single conversation might spark confidence, clarity, or courage in ways you can't yet imagine. By embracing the spirit of mentorship, you join a tradition of shared growth and empowerment, proving that none of us have to walk this journey alone.

PART 5 CREATING SAFE SPACES: ENCOURAGING OPEN DIALOGUE

Arriving home and walking into your living room after a long day, your shoulders heavy with the weight of unspoken fears and frustrations. As you take a seat, you're greeted with warm smiles and nods of understanding. The energy in the room is palpable, an unspoken agreement that here, you can exhale, shed your defenses, and simply be. This is the essence of a safe space: a haven where your voice matters, your story is honored, and your vulnerability is met with empathy, not judgment. In such environments, inclusivity becomes the foundation, empathy the bridge, and confidentiality the unwavering promise that allows trust to flourish.

Open dialogue is the lifeblood of any thriving community. Through honest and transparent conversation, trust is built, and understanding is deepened. Encouraging diverse perspectives isn't just beneficial, it's essential. When different voices and experiences are brought to the table, the community becomes richer, more dynamic, and more reflective of the world we live in. Promoting empathy and active listening enhances this dialogue, as members learn to truly hear one another, bridging gaps and dissolving misunderstandings. By fostering an atmosphere where everyone feels comfortable sharing their thoughts, a community can grow in harmony, celebrating its diversity while working toward common goals.

Now, here's Olivia, a woman who joined a local support group after losing her job. At first, she was hesitant to share, worried about how her struggles might be perceived. But as she listened to others speak candidly about their fears and setbacks, she found the courage to open up. Instead of judgment, she was met with nods of encouragement and shared experiences. That safe space became her lifeline, helping her rebuild her confidence and take the first steps toward a new career. Olivia's story demonstrates how safe spaces can transform hesitation into empowerment, proving the healing power of open dialogue and inclusivity.

Creating a safe space begins with clearly defined community norms. Collaboratively develop these norms with members, ensuring that everyone has a voice in shaping the group's values. For instance, guidelines might include "respect all perspectives," "practice active listening," and "honor confidentiality." Display these norms visibly during gatherings or post them in online communities as a reminder of the shared commitment. Inclusivity can also be encouraged by celebrating diversity within the group. Acknowledge and honor different cultural backgrounds, life experiences, and perspectives, creating an environment where differences are seen as strengths. Facilitators can model inclusivity by actively seeking input from quieter participants, ensuring that every voice is heard and valued.

Safe spaces are not created by accident, they are built intentionally, nurtured with empathy, and sustained through mutual respect. By fostering environments where authenticity thrives and every voice is heard, we contribute to communities that uplift and empower. Whether you're establishing norms, encouraging dialogue, or simply listening with an open heart, your efforts ripple outward, creating bonds that transform individual struggles into collective strength. As we move into the next chapter, we'll explore how adopting a growth mindset can further enhance your ability to cultivate resilience and possibility, both within yourself and within the communities you cherish.

CHAPTER 6

Embracing a Growth Mindset

"BECOMING IS BETTER THAN BEING." CAROL DWECK

Maria stood at the edge of a crossroads, her thoughts racing as the city buzzed around her. Her dream of starting her own business felt thrilling but overwhelming. Doubts whispered in her mind: *"What if I fail?" "What if I'm not ready?"* She had always played it safe, choosing paths where she knew the outcome. But something inside her stirred, a small, determined voice urging her to take the leap. Maria realized this wasn't just a decision about her career; it was a choice about her mindset. Was she willing to see herself as someone who could grow, learn, and adapt? Or would she let fear and self-doubt keep her stuck?

This moment reflects the essence of a growth mindset, the belief that abilities can be developed through effort, strategies, and a willingness to learn. A growth mindset reframes challenges as opportunities for growth, transforming hesitation into progress. In contrast, a fixed mindset, which sees talents as unchangeable, often leads to self-doubt, avoidance of challenges, and stagnation. Maria's story is an invitation to embrace a growth mindset, redefine how you view obstacles, and discover the limitless possibilities that lie beyond your comfort zone.

A growth mindset isn't just a philosophy; it's a transformative approach to life. When you adopt this perspective, challenges become paths forward rather than roadblocks. Instead of avoiding difficulties, you engage with them, viewing setbacks as opportunities to learn and improve. This shift fosters creativity and problem-solving, equipping you to tackle obstacles with resilience and determination. Resilience becomes your ally, helping you bounce back stronger from failures and approach life with courage. With a growth mindset, learning becomes a lifelong journey, enriching your personal and professional experiences.

To nurture a growth mindset, start by viewing challenges as opportunities to discover something new. When difficulties arise, pause and ask yourself, *What lesson can I learn here? How can this help me grow?* This practice shifts your perspective from the problem to the possibilities, encouraging you to explore creative solutions. As we analyze Maria's journey, we see that she began by breaking her goal into smaller steps, each one building her confidence and skill set. With each small success, her belief in her ability to grow strengthened.

Seeking feedback is another powerful way to cultivate growth. Think about a time when you received constructive criticism, perhaps from a colleague or a mentor. How did you react? Feedback can feel uncomfortable, but it is an invaluable tool for refinement. Instead of seeing it as a personal critique, frame it as guidance to help you improve. Ask questions, reflect, and use the insights to sharpen your skills. Feedback, when embraced, becomes a bridge to greater self-awareness and progress.

Effort is another cornerstone of a growth mindset. Recognize that persistence is not a sign of struggle but a hallmark of progress. Each attempt, even the ones that don't succeed, strengthens your foundation. Acknowledge the small victories along the way, finishing a project, learning a new skill, or even stepping out of your comfort zone for the first time. These moments, though small, build the perseverance and confidence necessary for larger achievements.

Growth happens when you dare to try something new. Whether it's signing up for a pottery class, tackling a new project at work, or speaking up in a meeting, every step outside your comfort zone is a step toward discovering more about yourself. Maria found this to be true when she began attending networking events to connect with other entrepreneurs. At first, she felt out of place, unsure of how to share her ideas. But over time, these experiences taught her to communicate her vision with confidence, and she began forming meaningful connections that propelled her dream forward.

Similarly, embracing experimentation and risk-taking in your daily life can unlock new opportunities. Try a new recipe, explore a different route on your morning walk, or sign up for a class that intrigues you. These activities foster curiosity and adaptability, helping you build confidence in your ability to navigate the unknown. In the workplace, try volunteering for a project that challenges your current skills. While the experience may feel daunting, it will stretch your capabilities and open doors to growth.

Interactive Element: Growth Mindset Reflection Exercise

Take a moment to reflect on your own journey. Think about a recent challenge or opportunity you encountered and ask yourself these questions:

1. Did I approach this situation as a chance to grow, or did I let fear hold me back?
2. What feedback did I receive, and how can I use it constructively?
3. What effort or action can I take today to build momentum toward my goals?

Write down your responses in a journal or notebook. Revisit them as you continue to cultivate your growth mindset. Each reflection brings clarity and strengthens your resolve to embrace growth, one step at a time. Through this process, you'll discover that the most rewarding moments in life often begin with the courage to choose growth over fear.

PART 1 OVERCOMING PERFECTIONISM: EMBRACING IMPERFECTION

Perfectionism often masquerades as a virtue, but beneath its polished exterior lies a mindset that can stifle creativity and hinder growth. It lures you into setting impossibly high standards, whispering that anything less than flawless is a failure. Over time, this pursuit of perfection becomes a weight, breeding fear of mistakes and trapping you in cycles of procrastination and self-doubt. Decisions feel paralyzed under the looming shadow of imperfection, making it difficult to start projects, share ideas, or take risks. Instead of viewing mistakes as opportunities for growth, perfectionism convinces you they are signs of inadequacy, halting progress before it even begins.

Yet, imperfection is not the enemy, it is the foundation of growth. When you embrace your flaws and allow room for mistakes, you unlock creativity and innovation. True progress happens when you step into the unknown, unburdened by the need for everything to be perfect. This mindset grants you the freedom to experiment, to take risks, and to learn from both success and failure. By viewing imperfection as an integral part of the process, you shift your priority from achieving unattainable ideals to cultivating resilience and curiosity. It's here, in the messy and imperfect moments, that true breakthroughs and discoveries emerge.

To break free from the grip of perfectionism, start by setting realistic goals that prioritize progress over perfection. Break down overwhelming tasks into smaller, manageable steps. For example, instead of expecting to write the perfect report in one sitting, aim to complete an outline or draft, allowing space for refinement later. Celebrate small victories as milestones, acknowledging that each step forward is a meaningful contribution to your larger goals. By homing in on incremental progress, you build momentum and confidence, reducing the paralyzing pressure to achieve perfection right away.

Self-compassion is another critical tool in overcoming perfectionism. When you make a mistake, treat yourself with kindness rather than harsh criticism. Remind yourself that errors are a universal part of being human, and often the greatest teachers. Practicing self-forgiveness allows you to move forward with a lighter heart, cultivating a supportive inner dialogue that encourages growth rather than fear. For instance, when a project doesn't go as planned, instead of fixating on what went wrong, ask yourself, "What did I learn from this experience?" This simple shift in perspective reframes mistakes as building blocks, reinforcing the idea that imperfection is a natural part of progress.

Journaling can be a powerful practice for dismantling perfectionist tendencies. Use your journal to document small successes, lessons learned, and moments of growth. Reflect on questions like, "What progress am I proud of today?" or "What did I learn from a recent challenge?" These reflections create a record of your resilience and evolution, reminding you that growth is a journey, not a destination. Over time, this habit builds a narrative of self-acceptance and progress, countering the inner voice that demands flawlessness.

Experimentation and risk-taking are also essential in loosening perfectionism's grip. Allow yourself to try new things, even if you don't excel right away. Whether it's painting for the first time, learning a new language, or tackling a challenging project at work, stepping outside your comfort zone fosters adaptability and creativity. Each attempt, regardless of outcome, teaches you something valuable. The act of trying becomes more important than achieving perfection, allowing you to engage with life more fully and joyfully.

Finally, shift your target from perfection to the process itself. Growth happens in the messy, imperfect moments, in drafts that aren't quite right, in ideas that fail, and in the moments where you feel stretched and uncertain. By embracing imperfection, you free yourself from the suffocating need for flawless execution, opening the door to exploration and possibility.

Letting go of perfectionism doesn't mean lowering your standards, it means recognizing that excellence is born from effort, adaptability, and persistence, not from unattainable ideals. It's about accepting yourself fully, with all your strengths and flaws, and understanding that imperfection is a powerful force for growth. When you release the pressure to be perfect, you allow yourself to flourish, creating a life enriched by curiosity, resilience, and the courage to embrace your most authentic self.

PART 2 LEARNING FROM FAILURE: TURNING SETBACKS INTO SETUPS

Failure is not an endpoint; it's an opportunity and a foundation for growth and discovery. Think back to a moment when something you planned didn't go the way you envisioned. The disappointment likely stung, perhaps filling you with frustration or self-doubt. But what if you could view that moment not as a defeat, but as a crucial lesson? What if failure, instead of being the end of the road, became a detour pointing you toward a better path? This shift in perspective transforms failure into a tool for growth, a guide that highlights what didn't work and reveals what could. By embracing failure as feedback, you begin to see it not as a road-block, but as a bridge to success.

History brims with examples of individuals who have transformed setbacks into setups for success. Contend with the story of an entrepreneur whose first business venture ended in bankruptcy. While devastating at the time, that failure provided invaluable lessons about risk management and strategy. Armed with those insights, they launched a second, more successful enterprise, achieving even greater heights. Or take the story of an artist whose early work was met with rejection after rejection. Rather than giving up, they allowed those "no's" to fuel their creativity, exploring new techniques that ultimately defined their signature style and gained widespread acclaim. These stories remind us that every failure carries within it the seeds of transformation, pushing us to adapt, innovate, and persevere.

To transform failure into a learning opportunity, start by adopting a process of reflection and analysis. Conduct a "post-mortem" of the situation, treating it as an experiment from which you can extract valuable insights. Ask yourself: "What went wrong?" "What factors contributed to this outcome?" and "What could I have done differently?" This step isn't about assigning blame, either to yourself or others, it's about gaining clarity. By examining the situation objectively, you can identify the root causes of failure and pinpoint areas for improvement. This deliberate reflection turns a setback into a source of actionable knowledge, equipping you with the tools to make better decisions moving forward.

Once you've analyzed the missteps, spotlight your intensity on creating a roadmap for improvement. Identify specific, actionable changes you can implement to prevent similar outcomes in the future. This might involve refining your skills, seeking additional resources, or approaching challenges from a different angle. For instance, if a failed presentation was due to a lack of preparation, you might commit to rehearsing more thoroughly next time. Or, if a business venture faltered due to insufficient market research, you could make more informed, data-driven decisions in the future. These adjustments, however small, lay the groundwork for future success, ensuring that failure becomes a smooth path rather than a stumbling block.

The lessons of failure are not theoretical; they are embedded in countless real-world stories. How about this story of an athlete who didn't make the cut for their dream team. Instead of giving up, they used that disappointment as motivation to train harder, eventually becoming a champion in their sport. Or the scientist whose groundbreaking discovery came only after years of experiments that didn't yield the desired results. Each setback wasn't a failure but a vital piece of the puzzle, helping them refine their approach and get closer to the breakthrough. These stories are not just inspiring, they're evidence that setbacks are often disguised as opportunities for growth and reinvention.

Resilience and persistence are the cornerstones of learning from failure. Developing these qualities helps you face challenges with courage and determination. A robust support system can make all the difference. Surround yourself with people who believe in your potential and who offer encouragement and constructive feedback when you stumble. This network of mentors, friends, and peers can serve as a wellspring of strength, providing perspective and reminding you of your capabilities when self-doubt threatens to creep in. Their belief in you acts as a buffer against discouragement, helping you stay oriented on the lessons rather than the losses.

Additionally, cultivate personal rituals or mantras to keep you grounded during difficult moments. For instance, a phrase like "Every failure is a step forward" or "I am growing through this challenge" can serve as a powerful reminder of your resilience. These affirmations anchor you in the belief that setbacks are temporary and that your efforts will ultimately lead to progress. By developing a habit of resilience and self-compassion, you can face failure with greater confidence, turning each stumble into an opportunity for self-discovery and growth.

Ultimately, failure is a teacher, a necessary companion on the road to success. It reveals hidden weaknesses, sharpens your skills, and strengthens your resolve. By reframing failure as a source of feedback rather than a personal shortcoming, you empower yourself to grow, adapt, and persevere. Each setback becomes a setup, preparing you for the challenges and triumphs ahead. And as you continue to embrace failure as part of the process, you'll find that it's not the end of your journey but the beginning of something even greater.

PART 3 REAL-LIFE EXAMPLES: GROWTH MINDSET IN ACTION

In the world of athletics, there's a powerful story about Janelle, a sprinter whose dreams nearly unraveled after a career-threatening injury. The moment she heard the diagnosis, a torn Achilles tendon, Janelle felt her world come to a halt. The track, her second home, suddenly felt out of reach. But instead of surrendering to despair, Janelle chose a different path. She saw her injury not as the end of her career but as a new challenge to overcome. With a determined mindset, she dove into rehabilitation, channeling each physical therapy session as a chance to rebuild her strength. She tracked her progress meticulously, celebrated small victories, and embraced new techniques her coaches introduced. Slowly but steadily, Janelle returned to the track, not just healed but stronger than before. In her first major race post-injury, she shattered her previous personal record, a testament to her resilience and growth. Janelle's journey reminds us that setbacks can become springboards when we approach them with openness and determination.

Another story of transformation comes from Marisol, a student who once struggled to keep up in math class. Numbers felt like an insurmountable wall, and every wrong answer seemed to reinforce her belief that she was "just not a math person." But one day, a teacher encouraged her to view mistakes as clues rather than failures. Inspired, Marisol began seeking help from tutors, watching online videos, and practicing diligently. Every error became an opportunity to refine her understanding. Over time, her hard work paid off. Not only did she improve her grades, but she also discovered a love for problem-solving. Years later, Marisol pursued a degree in engineering, using the same growth mindset that had transformed her early struggles into a lifelong passion for learning. Her story demonstrates how the way we frame challenges can shape not only our abilities but also our future.

Both Janelle and Marisol's journeys highlight the transformative power of a growth mindset. At the core of their success was an unwavering commitment to continuous improvement. They viewed feedback as a tool for growth, not a critique of their worth, and embraced challenges as opportunities to stretch their capabilities. Their willingness to adapt and persist allowed them to achieve outcomes that once seemed impossible.

The impact of their growth mindsets reached far beyond their initial goals. For Janelle, the discipline, resilience, and strategic thinking she developed during her recovery enriched other areas of her life, from mentoring younger athletes to navigating personal challenges with newfound confidence. Marisol's academic transformation didn't just change her grades, it altered the trajectory of her life, paving the way for a career she once thought unattainable. These stories illustrate that a growth mindset isn't confined to a single goal or moment; it's a way of approaching life that fosters ongoing growth and fulfillment.

As you dwell on these examples, think about how you might apply the same principles to your own challenges. Ask yourself: *"What setbacks have I faced recently, and what lessons can I extract from them?" "How can I reframe these experiences as opportunities for growth?" "What small steps can I take today to move closer to my goals?"* Whether you're recovering from a personal disappointment or tackling a professional hurdle, adopting a growth-oriented perspective can unlock doors you never knew existed. Embrace the discomfort of learning, seek feedback with curiosity, and trust that every effort you make is building a foundation for future success.

PART 4 WORKSHOPS AND RESOURCES: TOOLS FOR CONTINUOUS IMPROVEMENT

Step into a space buzzing with energy, people exchanging ideas, practicing new skills, and pushing the boundaries of their understanding. This is the magic of workshops. These immersive experiences go beyond lectures; they offer hands-on activities, real-time discussions, and the chance to network with others who share your interests. Whether it's a one-day seminar or a week-long masterclass, workshops provide the tools and inspiration needed to ignite curiosity and spark growth. The collaborative atmosphere fosters creativity as participants learn from both experts and peers. By the end, you leave not just with new knowledge but with practical skills and meaningful connections that enrich your personal and professional life.

In the digital realm, learning opportunities are limitless. Online courses, podcasts, and webinars allow you to learn at your own pace, making education more accessible than ever. You can tune into a podcast while sipping your morning coffee, join a live webinar from your desk, or explore a course during a quiet evening. These resources bring global experts to your fingertips, offering insights that can challenge your perspectives and deepen your expertise. Platforms like Coursera, Udemy, or TED Talks provide options for structured learning, while podcasts and YouTube channels deliver bite-sized knowledge that fits seamlessly into a busy schedule. By embracing digital tools, you gain the flexibility to expand your horizons no matter where you are.

With so many options available, choosing the right resources can feel overwhelming. Start by clarifying your goals, what do you want to achieve, and what skills or knowledge will help you get there? Look for resources that align with these objectives and have strong reviews or recommendations. For example, if you want to improve your public speaking skills, enrolling in a Toastmasters workshop or an online course like "The Art of Public Speaking." By being intentional in your selections, you ensure that each learning experience has a meaningful impact on your growth.

Lifelong learning is essential in today's rapidly evolving world. As industries transform and technologies advance, staying informed is key to remaining competitive and adaptable. Beyond career advancement, continuous learning fosters personal growth, helping you stay curious and engaged. It's not just about acquiring knowledge but about cultivating a mindset that welcomes change and thrives on discovery. This adaptable mindset enables you to approach challenges as opportunities for growth, keeping you resilient and prepared for whatever the future may hold.

To make learning a consistent part of your life, develop a personal learning plan. Start by identifying specific, measurable goals. For instance, you might decide to improve your creative writing skills by completing a course on storytelling or attending a monthly writer's workshop. Create a weekly schedule that includes dedicated time for learning, whether it's 20 minutes of daily reading, an hour-long podcast each week, or a quarterly in-person seminar. Balance formal education with informal exploration, like watching educational videos or experimenting with a new hobby. By weaving learning into your routine, you not only enhance your skills but also nurture a lifelong love for discovery.

Workshops and online resources are more than tools for gaining knowledge, they're pathways to transformation. By immersing yourself in these opportunities and embracing continuous learning, you equip yourself to navigate life's challenges with confidence and creativity. Whether through a shared classroom experience or the quiet mindset of a webinar, every moment you invest in growth is a step toward becoming the best version of yourself.

PART 5 REFRAMING NEGATIVE THOUGHTS: THE POWER OF PERSPECTIVE

Negative thoughts, like unwelcome shadows, can quietly shape your mindset and influence your actions. They sow doubt, convincing you that you're not capable or deserving of success. Left unchecked, these thoughts spiral into self-fulfilling prophecies, keeping you stuck in a loop of inaction and self-doubt. For example, if you repeatedly tell yourself, "I'll never succeed," you're less likely to take the risks or make the effort required to achieve your goals. This cycle can be suffocating, but it doesn't have to define you. Recognizing the influence of negative thoughts is the first step toward regaining control over your perspective.

Changing your outlook begins with intentional strategies that help you reframe negativity. Cognitive restructuring is one powerful technique. Start by identifying unhelpful thoughts and questioning their accuracy. For instance, if you think, "I'm always failing," take a moment to reflect on your successes, no matter how small. Replace that thought with a more constructive one, such as, "I've faced challenges before and found ways to succeed." Visualization can amplify this shift, project a vision of yourself accomplishing your goals with confidence, vividly imagining the emotions and results. This practice trains your mind to gravitate toward possibilities rather than limitations, paving the way for optimism and action.

Gratitude journaling is another transformative tool. By writing down moments of gratitude each day, whether it's the warmth of the morning sun or a kind gesture from a friend, you gradually retrain your mind to see the need to stay positive. Over time, these small acknowledgments create a reservoir of positivity that can counteract negativity. Even on difficult days, this practice serves as a reminder that there is always something to appreciate, shifting your perspective from scarcity to abundance.

Mindfulness plays a pivotal role in addressing negative thought patterns. Through mindfulness meditation, you can observe your thoughts without judgment, allowing you to recognize and disengage from negative narratives as they arise. This practice helps create a mental pause, giving you the freedom to choose how to respond rather than reacting automatically. Reflective journaling complements mindfulness by encouraging you to explore the root causes of your negative thoughts. Ask yourself questions like, "Why do I believe this about myself?" or "What evidence do I have that contradicts this thought?" This process fosters clarity and self-awareness, equipping you to address negativity at its source.

Think through the story of Natasha, a professional grappling with imposter syndrome despite her impressive accomplishments. For years, she felt like a fraud, convinced her success was due to luck rather than ability. To combat these feelings, Natasha began practicing positive self-talk. Each morning, she reminded herself of her achievements, writing down affirmations like, "I earned my place, and I bring value to my work." Gradually, her confidence grew, and she began to see herself as the capable professional others had always recognized her to be. Similarly, James, a high school student struggling with self-doubt, used affirmations to shift his mindset. By repeating, "I am capable and improving every day," he found the courage to approach challenges with determination, ultimately excelling in subjects he once feared.

These stories demonstrate the profound power of reframing your perspective. When you shift your mindset, obstacles become opportunities, and failures become lessons. It's not about denying difficulties but about choosing to view them as steps on the path to growth. By embracing strategies like cognitive restructuring, gratitude journaling, and mindfulness, you cultivate resilience and open yourself to a world of possibilities.

The journey to a positive mindset is ongoing, but it begins with a single step. Today, choose one strategy to try, whether it's identifying and challenging a negative belief, listing three things you're grateful for, or spending five minutes in mindful reflection. Each small action brings you closer to a more empowered, fulfilled version of yourself.

CHAPTER 7

Practicing Mindfulness and Presence

> "Feelings come and go like clouds in a windy sky. Conscious breathing is my anchor."
>
> *THICH NHAT HANH*

The noise of modern life can feel relentless, notifications buzzing, emails piling up, and thoughts racing through your mind like an unending stream. You're physically present at dinner but mentally replaying a meeting from earlier or planning tomorrow's to-do list. In this swirl of activity, finding calm might feel impossible. Yet within this chaos lies an antidote: mindfulness. Far from being a luxury or trend, mindfulness is an invitation to reclaim your attention and anchor yourself in the present. It's not just about being in the moment, it's about embracing it fully, with awareness, acceptance, and curiosity.

At its essence, mindfulness is the practice of observing your thoughts, emotions, and sensations without judgment. It's about seeing your experiences as they are, not as you wish them to be.

This clarity creates space for self-acceptance, quieting the critical inner voice that often adds to stress. Acceptance, a cornerstone of mindfulness, encourages you to meet each moment with openness, using it as a starting point for thoughtful action rather than resistance. Most importantly, mindfulness brings you back to the present, helping you let go of past regrets and future anxieties. This magnetic view of "the now" becomes a refuge, allowing you to engage fully with life as it unfolds.

Staying present, however, is easier said than done. In today's hyper-connected world, distractions are everywhere. The ping of a notification pulls you away mid-conversation, and the demands of multitasking scatter your thoughts across a dozen unfinished tasks. These constant interruptions create a sense of disconnection, not just from others but from yourself. You may feel like you're always moving but never truly present. Over time, this fragmented attention takes a toll, leaving you stressed, unfocused, and exhausted. Yet mindfulness offers a way to pause the noise and reclaim your inner stillness.

The benefits of mindfulness are both profound and well-documented. By practicing mindfulness, you can reduce stress and anxiety, cultivating a calm center even in the midst of chaos. Techniques like deep breathing or meditation bring your attention back to the present, soothing the mind and quieting worry. As you strengthen your ability to orient yourself, you'll notice an increased capacity for concentration and efficiency, whether at work or in personal tasks. Mindfulness also enhances emotional resilience, teaching you to observe feelings without becoming consumed by them. This newfound balance allows you to respond to challenges with clarity and composure, improving both your mental and emotional well-being.

Incorporating mindfulness into your daily life doesn't require dramatic changes, just small, intentional moments. Begin by setting a personal mindfulness mantra, a simple phrase that reminds you to stay present. It could be as simple as "I am here, now" or "Each moment matters." Use this mantra as an anchor, repeating it whenever your mind begins to wander. Daily prompts, like setting a gentle alarm on your phone or placing sticky notes in visible spots, can help you pause for mindful moments. These reminders allow you to reset, reconnecting with the present even amidst a busy day.

Mindfulness thrives in simplicity. Start with a practice as small as taking three deep breaths before beginning a task. In those moments, refine your awareness entirely on the sensation of breathing, the rise and fall of your chest, the flow of air through your nostrils. This brief pause can reset your mind, bringing calm and clarity to whatever comes next. Whether it's a mindful walk where you notice the rhythm of your steps or a gratitude reflection before bed, each small act of presence adds up, creating a more peaceful and intentional life.

Interactive Element: Craft Your Mindfulness Mantra

Reflect on what mindfulness means to you and create a mantra that encapsulates your intention to stay present. Perhaps it's "I am grounded in this moment," or "Breathe in peace, breathe out stress." Write it down and place it somewhere prominent, your desk, your phone background, or your bathroom mirror. Let this mantra become a guide, gently bringing you back to the present whenever your thoughts wander.

Mindfulness isn't about perfection; it's about practice. Each moment spent in awareness is a victory, a step closer to a calmer and more intentional life. Begin today with a single breath, a single pause, and see how the ripple effects unfold in your day. The present moment is always waiting to welcome you back, one mindful step at a time.

PART 1 PRACTICAL MINDFULNESS TECHNIQUES: FROM MEDITATION TO BREATHING

Life can feel like a whirlwind, endless notifications, crowded schedules, and thoughts racing from one worry to the next. But amidst the busyness, moments of peace are within reach. Mindfulness invites you to slow down, reconnect with yourself, and find stillness in the present. Meditation, a cornerstone of mindfulness, offers a gateway to this calm. With no one-size-fits-all approach, it encompasses a range of techniques to suit different needs. Focused attention meditation sharpens your concentration by anchoring your awareness to a single point, like your breath or a repeated mantra. Loving-kindness meditation expands your capacity for compassion, encouraging you to send goodwill to yourself and others. The body scan method, meanwhile, fosters relaxation by guiding your awareness through each part of your body, helping you release tension and tune into physical sensations. Each technique holds unique benefits, making it easy to tailor your practice to your personal goals and preferences.

Starting a meditation practice doesn't require grand gestures, it begins with simplicity. Find a quiet space, free from distractions. It could be a cozy corner of your living room or even a park bench during a peaceful moment. Set a timer for just five minutes. As you sit, let your attention settle on your breath, noticing the gentle rhythm of inhalation and exhalation. Your thoughts may wander, and that's okay, simply guide your mind's eye back to your breathing each time. This practice of returning to the present builds patience and resilience over time, forming the foundation for deeper mindfulness. Whether practiced daily or occasionally, these small steps can cultivate a sense of calm that carries through your day.

Breathing exercises are another powerful tool for grounding yourself and cultivating mindfulness. Diaphragmatic breathing, or belly breathing, invites you to take deep, full breaths that expand your diaphragm, calming your nervous system and easing tension. With box breathing, you follow a structured rhythm: inhale for four counts, hold for four, exhale for four, and hold again for four. This technique, popular among high-stress professionals, steadies both the body and mind. For balance and calm, alternate nostril breathing guides you to inhale through one nostril and exhale through the other, creating harmony between mind and body. Each technique offers a unique pathway to relaxation, inviting you to explore and find the one that resonates most with you.

Discovering which mindfulness practices suit you best is a journey of experimentation. Guided meditations can provide structure and support, with soothing instructions that lead you through each step, while unguided practices give you the freedom to explore at your own pace. Apps like Headspace and Calm offer a wealth of resources, including meditations tailored to goals like stress reduction, better sleep, or improved sharpness. These tools allow you to practice anytime, anywhere, with features like progress tracking and gentle reminders to help you stay consistent. Whether you're a beginner or looking to deepen your practice, these resources can bring mindfulness into even the busiest schedules.

As you incorporate mindfulness into your daily life, remember that there's no right or wrong way to practice. What matters is finding techniques that feel natural and meaningful to you. Lay a small foundation: take a moment to close your eyes and breathe deeply before a meeting, or dedicate five minutes to a guided meditation before bed. These simple acts of presence can transform your day, helping you feel calmer, more focused, and more in tune with yourself. Mindfulness isn't about perfection, it's about progress. With each breath, each pause, you take a step closer to a life that feels balanced and fulfilling.

Interactive Element: Try a Breathing Exercise Today

Choose one of the breathing techniques described, diaphragmatic breathing, box breathing, or alternate nostril breathing, and dedicate two minutes to practicing it. Set a timer, find a comfortable space, and meditate fully on the rhythm of your breath. Reflect on how you feel afterward. Did it bring a sense of calm or clarity? Make a habit of adding this practice to your daily routine, creating moments of mindfulness that support your overall well-being.

PART 2 INCORPORATING MINDFULNESS INTO DAILY LIFE: SMALL STEPS, BIG IMPACT

Your day begins as an infographic, with each moment a pencil stroke drawing the story of your life. Mindfulness transforms these ordinary moments into opportunities for connection and presence, helping you savor the richness of your daily experiences. This approach, often called "mindful living," weaves awareness into your everyday routine, allowing you to appreciate life's nuances without setting aside time for formal practices. Take eating, for instance: instead of rushing through meals, slow down. Let each bite become an exploration, notice the vibrant flavors, the unique textures, the comforting warmth. This simple act of attentiveness elevates eating from a task to a meditative experience, grounding you in the here and now.

Even activities as routine as walking can become opportunities for mindfulness. Become aligned with the rhythm of your steps, the sensations in your body, and the sounds and sights around you. Feel the ground beneath your feet and the breeze on your face. Instead of walking just to get somewhere, immerse yourself fully in the journey. Each step becomes a reminder to reconnect with your surroundings, cultivating a sense of calm and awareness that resonates throughout your day.

Incorporating mindfulness doesn't require dramatic changes to your schedule, it's about infusing the moments you already have with attention and care. During your commute, whether on a train, bus, or car, try observing the world around you. Notice the soft glow of the morning sun, the rhythm of passing cars, or the details in the scenery. Turn this time into an intentional pause, transforming the mundane into the meaningful. Even tidying your home can be a mindful act. View with intention on the sensations of cleaning, the feel of water on your hands, the smell of fresh laundry, the satisfaction of creating order. These everyday moments, approached with intention, become meditative practices, bringing peace and serenity to your day.

Small, consistent acts of mindfulness accumulate, creating a ripple effect that enhances your emotional resilience and overall well-being. Even a few moments of presence can reduce stress, sharpen your vision, and strengthen your ability to handle life's challenges with grace. Over time, you may notice yourself becoming more patient, centered, and attuned to the world around you. This deepened connection enriches your experience of life, turning the ordinary into the extraordinary.

To anchor mindfulness in your routine, consider using cues as gentle reminders to pause and refocus. The sound of birdsong, the warmth of a morning coffee, or even the sensation of water while washing your hands can become signals to take a mindful breath. Habit stacking, linking mindfulness to regular activities like brushing your teeth or waiting in line, further reinforces this practice. You might even set subtle phone alerts that encourage you to pause and re-center throughout the day. By blending mindfulness into the fabric of your daily life, you cultivate a practice that is simple yet transformative, infusing every moment with purpose, presence, and peace.

PART 3 GUIDED PRACTICES: AUDIO AND VIDEO RESOURCES FOR MINDFULNESS

Contemplate sinking into a cozy chair at the end of a demanding day, ready to quiet your mind and unwind. This is where guided mindfulness practices become a sanctuary, gently leading you into relaxation and heightened awareness. These tools are designed to make mindfulness approachable for all, whether you're just beginning your journey or seeking to deepen an established routine. For beginners, guided sessions offer reassurance and structure, removing the guesswork and allowing you to simply immerse yourself in the experience. For seasoned practitioners, they bring variety and fresh perspectives, keeping your practice dynamic and engaging.

Today's digital landscape is rich with mindfulness resources that cater to every need and lifestyle. Apps like *Insight Timer* boast an expansive library of meditations, from quick five-minute resets to longer, immersive experiences for deep relaxation. *Smiling Mind* stands out for its simplicity and warmth, offering a straightforward approach that resonates with both younger users and those seeking an accessible introduction to mindfulness. Prefer video content? Platforms like YouTube host exceptional channels such as *Yoga with Adriene* and *The Honest Guys*. These creators provide a variety of sessions, ranging from calming yoga flows to deeply restorative meditations, making mindfulness available at the click of a button.

The beauty of guided practices lies in their versatility. Feeling restless at night? Guided sleep meditations gently lead you into a tranquil state, their soothing tones and imagery quieting your mind as you drift into restful sleep. Starting your morning with a positive mindset can be supported by energizing morning meditations that set your intentions for the day ahead. When stress feels overwhelming, stress-relief sessions offer immediate comfort, helping you release tension and find your equilibrium. Each type of guided session is crafted to meet specific needs, ensuring that no matter the situation, there's a practice to ground and uplift you.

To integrate guided mindfulness into your life, create a personalized playlist tailored to your unique needs and preferences. Think of this playlist as a toolkit: a calming sleep meditation to wind down at night, a short midday practice to reset during a busy workday, and a longer relaxation session for moments when you need deeper grounding. Curating your playlist allows you to have mindfulness practices at your fingertips, ready to support you whenever you need them. Scheduling regular sessions, whether it's a morning ritual, a mid-afternoon breather, or a pre-bedtime routine, helps build consistency, making mindfulness a natural and rewarding part of your daily life.

Interactive Element: Create Your Mindfulness Playlist

Explore a variety of guided resources, from meditation apps to YouTube videos, and note which ones resonate most with you. Organize your favorites into a playlist by theme, sleep, energy, stress relief, or time of day. Use this playlist as your personal sanctuary, a collection of practices that support your journey toward greater peace and presence. Whether it's a quick reset or a longer session, your playlist will be a reliable companion, ready to guide you back to balance whenever life feels overwhelming.

PART 4 THE ROLE OF SELF-COMPASSION: BEING KIND TO YOURSELF

Think of how you'd speak to a close friend during a difficult time, you'd likely offer understanding, kindness, and words of encouragement. Now, take a look at turning that same compassion inward. This is the essence of self-compassion: treating yourself with the same empathy and warmth you'd naturally extend to others. It's built on three foundational pillars: self-kindness, common humanity, and mindfulness. Self-kindness involves speaking to yourself with gentleness, especially during moments of failure or difficulty, replacing harsh self-criticism with words of support. Common humanity reminds us that mistakes and struggles are part of the shared human experience, a universal truth that connects us all. Also, mindfulness allows you to observe your emotions without judgment, acknowledging pain without being consumed by it. Together, these principles create a nurturing space for healing, growth, and acceptance.

The mental health benefits of self-compassion are profound. By softening the voice of inner criticism, self-compassion reduces stress and promotes emotional resilience. It teaches you to recover more easily from setbacks, approaching challenges with patience rather than harsh judgment. When you embrace self-compassion, you cultivate a deep sense of inner peace, a reminder that you are enough as you are, without needing to prove your worth through perfection or achievement. In a world that often equates value with productivity, self-compassion offers a much-needed sanctuary, encouraging you to honor your humanity and find strength in vulnerability. This shift not only enhances your emotional well-being but also radiates outward, enriching your relationships by fostering greater empathy and connection.

Practicing self-compassion can feel unfamiliar at first, but simple exercises can help you cultivate this powerful mindset. Loving-kindness meditation is a beautiful way to begin. Find a quiet place where you can sit comfortably. Close your eyes, take a deep breath, and repeat phrases like, "May I be happy. May I be healthy. May I be at peace." These affirmations may feel awkward initially, but with time, they can soften the critical voice within and encourage a more nurturing self-dialogue. Journaling is another transformative tool. Write yourself a letter as though you were speaking to a friend who is facing the same struggles you are. Offer words of understanding and reassurance, acknowledge your challenges, and remind yourself of your strengths. This practice not only shifts your perspective but also fosters a sense of clarity, helping you approach difficulties with greater kindness and perspective.

Blending self-compassion with mindfulness practices can deepen your emotional resilience. During meditation, pay attention to any negative thoughts or emotions that arise. Instead of pushing them away, meet them with curiosity and kindness, as though you were offering comfort to a friend. At the end of your meditation, take a moment to reflect on the effort you've invested in caring for yourself. Place a hand over your heart, take a deep breath, and silently thank yourself for prioritizing your well-being. These small gestures of gratitude can reinforce the practice of self-compassion, creating a supportive inner environment where healing and growth can flourish.

Interactive Element: A Self-Compassion Check-In

Take a moment to reflect on how you speak to yourself during challenging times. Ask yourself:

1. When I face difficulty, do I treat myself with the same kindness I offer a loved one?
2. What words of reassurance could I say to myself right now?
3. How can I honor my shared humanity in this moment, reminding myself that imperfection is part of being human?

Take time to write down your reflections or speak them aloud, allowing this practice to guide you toward greater self-compassion.

PART 5 OVERCOMING RESISTANCE: MAKING MINDFULNESS A HABIT

Many people approach mindfulness with the best intentions but struggle to make it a lasting habit. One of the most common obstacles is the belief that there simply isn't enough time. Between deadlines, family responsibilities, and social commitments, life can feel like a never-ending race, leaving little room for stillness. In such a busy world, it's tempting to place mindfulness at the bottom of the priority list. Yet mindfulness doesn't require hours of quiet meditation; it's about weaving brief moments of presence into your day. Even pausing for a single mindful breath while waiting at a stoplight or brewing your morning coffee can make a meaningful difference, anchoring you amidst the chaos.

Another challenge is the frustration of a wandering mind. In a world full of distractions, staying present can feel like an impossible task. You might find yourself replaying past conversations, planning the day ahead, or crafting mental to-do lists when you're trying to prioritize your breathing. These moments often lead to self-doubt and the false belief that you're "failing" at mindfulness. However, mindfulness isn't about achieving the perfect 20-20 vision; it's about noticing when your mind drifts and gently guiding it back. Each time you return to the present, you strengthen your ability to stay aware, like building muscle through repetition. It's not about doing it perfectly; it's about showing up.

To overcome these barriers, begin by setting small, realistic goals. Commit to just two minutes of mindful breathing or reflection each day, and gradually increase the time as you feel ready. This incremental approach helps you establish a habit without feeling overwhelmed. Creating a dedicated space for mindfulness can also make a big difference. It doesn't need to be elaborate, perhaps a quiet corner with a cushion or a cozy chair near a window. Having a consistent spot for your practice sends a signal to your brain that this is a time for calm and presence, helping you shift into a mindful mindset more easily.

Accountability can be another powerful motivator. Partner with a friend or family member who's also interested in mindfulness. Share your goals, compare experiences, and encourage each other to stay consistent. Even checking in with each other briefly each week can make the journey feel more connected and enjoyable. Practicing alongside someone else can also open you to new techniques and perspectives, enriching your understanding of what mindfulness can look like.

Most importantly, approach mindfulness with flexibility and self-compassion. There will be days when your practice feels effortless and others when your mind seems like it's running in every direction. Be kind to yourself during those harder moments, recognizing that mindfulness is a lifelong practice, not a destination. If your routine falters, give yourself permission to start again, adjusting your approach to fit your current needs. Some days, this might mean a five-minute meditation instead of ten. On other days, it might mean skipping a formal practice entirely and instead focusing on mindful moments, like savoring a cup of tea or taking a slow, intentional walk. The key is to keep coming back, however imperfectly.

Meditate on the story of Leah, a professional whose packed schedule left her feeling overwhelmed and unfocused. She began with just three minutes of mindfulness each morning, sitting quietly before the demands of the day began. Over time, she increased her practice, finding that these moments of presence improved her concentration and productivity at work. Similarly, Mark, a parent juggling the chaos of family life, started integrating mindfulness into small, daily tasks. He found calm by pausing for a deep breath while washing dishes or paying attention to the rhythm of his footsteps during morning errands. Both of these individuals demonstrate that, no matter how busy life may seem, mindfulness can be a transformative and accessible practice.

Interactive Element: A Mindfulness "Starter" Plan

If you're new to mindfulness or struggling to build consistency, try this simple plan:

1. **Morning Moment:** Begin your day with three mindful breaths before checking your phone or starting your routine.
2. **Daily Anchor:** Choose one activity, such as brushing your teeth, preparing a meal, or walking to your car, and commit to doing it mindfully today. Pay full attention to the sensations, sights, and sounds of the moment.
3. **Evening Reflection:** Before bed, take one minute to reflect on a moment you felt present today. Acknowledge your efforts, no matter how small, and thank yourself for prioritizing your well-being.

With small, consistent steps like these, you'll find that mindfulness naturally weaves into the fabric of your daily life, offering clarity and calm amidst the busyness.

CHAPTER 8

Designing Your Best Life

> "You're always with yourself, so you might as well enjoy the company."

DIANE VON FÜRSTENBERG

Now, see a visionary image of yourself standing in a sunlit room, surrounded by images and words that reflect your dreams and aspirations. These visuals aren't just decorations; they're a map of your future laid out on a vision board. Often called a dream board, this creative tool acts as a powerful motivator, translating your deepest desires into a tangible reminder of what you're working toward. By placing your goals in a physical or digital format, you bring clarity and perspective to your ambitions, bridging the gap between imagination and reality.

The process of creating a vision board is as personal as it is empowering. Start by gathering materials: magazines, printed images, quotes, scissors, glue, or even a blank digital canvas. As you sift through these resources, pay attention to the visuals and words that resonate with your soul, places you dream of visiting, affirmations that energize you, or symbols that represent the life you want to create. These elements are the building blocks of your board, capturing the essence of your vision. Once you've collected what speaks to you, arrange them on your board in a way that feels inspiring and harmonious. This act of assembly isn't just about aesthetics; it's a process of intention-setting, where each image or word becomes a declaration of your goals.

The power of vision boards lies in their ability to laser-focus your energy and motivation. Displaying your board where you'll see it daily, whether it's on your bedroom wall, your desk, or your phone screen, keeps your aspirations front and center. Every glance at the board becomes a moment of reconnection with your goals, reminding you of the life you're striving to create. Over time, this consistent visualization can subtly shape your decisions and actions, making you more attuned to opportunities that align with your dreams. Research suggests that this practice engages both your conscious and subconscious mind, helping bridge the gap between intention and achievement.

Vision boards are not static; they're dynamic tools that evolve alongside you. As your goals shift and grow, take time to update your board to reflect your current aspirations. You might replace images of achieved milestones with new dreams or rearrange elements to align with fresh priorities. Scheduling a monthly review of your board can deepen your connection to your goals, serving as both a moment of celebration for what you've accomplished and a space to refocus on what lies ahead. This regular practice of reflection and renewal ensures that your board remains a true and vibrant representation of the life you want to design.

Creating a vision board also offers emotional benefits. Beyond motivation, the act of dreaming and visualizing can cultivate hope and joy. The process invites you to dream of a future filled with possibility, fostering optimism and reducing stress. It allows you to visualize what excites and inspires you, shifting attention away from doubts or obstacles. Each glance at your board is a reminder that you are in control of your narrative, capable of crafting a life that aligns with your values and passions.

For those who prefer digital tools, creating a virtual vision board can be just as impactful. Platforms like Pinterest or Canva provide intuitive ways to design and customize your board, offering flexibility and the ability to access it anywhere. You can curate a collection of images, quotes, and ideas online, creating a dynamic and easily updated resource. Whether physical or digital, the key is to choose a format that resonates with you, ensuring your vision board becomes a meaningful and inspiring part of your life.

Interactive Element: Create Your Vision Board

Dedicate time this week to designing your vision board. Gather magazines, printed materials, or digital tools like Pinterest. Reflect on your goals, dreams, and the emotions you want to cultivate in your life. Select images, quotes, and symbols that resonate with your vision, arranging them in a way that feels inspiring. Once complete, place your board somewhere visible or save it as a phone or desktop background. Revisit it regularly, allowing it to anchor you in your aspirations and guide your steps forward.

PART 1 GOAL SETTING FOR SUCCESS: ALIGNING GOALS WITH VALUES

Think of waking up every day with the confidence that your actions are deeply aligned with what truly matters to you. This is the power of setting meaningful goals that reflect your core principles. When your aspirations stem from your values, they transcend being mere items on a checklist. Instead, they become sources of intrinsic motivation, driving you forward with purpose and fulfillment. Value-driven goals not only provide direction but also ensure that your efforts contribute to a life rich in authenticity and personal growth.

Crafting meaningful objectives begins with aligning them to what you hold most dear. To do this effectively, you can use the SMART framework: Specific, Measurable, Achievable, Relevant, and Time-bound. This method transforms abstract ideas into tangible actions, giving your ambitions structure and clarity. Start by reflecting on your core principles. Ask yourself questions like, "What inspires me to get out of bed each morning?" or "What do I want to be remembered for?" Once you've identified your guiding values, whether it's creativity, connection, personal growth, or helping others, use them as the foundation for setting your goals. For example, if creativity is a key value, a SMART goal might be: "Complete one painting every month for the next six months."

Understanding yourself is essential to setting impactful goals. Self-awareness allows you to identify aspirations that align not only with your values but also with your strengths, passions, and potential areas for growth. Reflect on times when you've felt the most accomplished or fulfilled. What activities or accomplishments brought you joy? What skills did you rely on? These reflections illuminate patterns that can guide your goal-setting process. For example, if you've always felt energized after teaching or mentoring, a goal rooted in sharing knowledge, such as hosting a workshop or writing a blog series, may resonate deeply. The more your goals align with who you are, the more naturally you'll pursue them.

While clarity and structure are important, staying flexible in your approach is just as vital. Life is full of twists and turns, and as you grow, your priorities may shift. Embrace this change as a natural part of evolution. Flexibility means recognizing when a goal no longer aligns with your current values and having the courage to adjust it. For instance, a career-focused goal might take a backseat to health or family goals during a major life transition. Rather than viewing these adjustments as setbacks, see them as opportunities to refine your path. This adaptability keeps your goals relevant and ensures they continue to serve your authentic self.

Being flexible doesn't mean abandoning your goals when challenges arise; it's about finding creative ways to navigate obstacles. If a strategy isn't working, consider alternative approaches. If a timeline feels too tight, adjust it without guilt. Reflect on how new experiences or unexpected events shape your aspirations, and adapt your plans accordingly. This resilience helps you maintain momentum while staying grounded in what matters most. By treating change as an ally rather than an adversary, you open the door to growth and discovery, ensuring your goals remain meaningful and attainable.

Through thoughtful alignment with your values, a commitment to self-awareness, and the courage to adapt, you can create a goal-setting process that empowers you to live with intention. As you move forward, remember that goal-setting is not about perfection; it's about progress. Each step you take, no matter how small, brings you closer to a life that reflects your deepest aspirations.

Interactive Element: Value-Based Goal Setting Exercise

Set aside 15 minutes to clarify your values and craft a SMART goal:

1. Write down your top three values (e.g., creativity, community, health).
2. Reflect on how each value could shape a meaningful goal in your life.
3. Choose one goal to zero-in on and make it SMART:
   - Specific: What exactly do you want to achieve?
   - Measurable: How will you track progress?
   - Achievable: Is this realistic given your resources and time?
   - Relevant: How does this goal align with your values?
   - Time-bound: When do you want to accomplish it?

Display your SMART goal somewhere visible, and revisit it regularly to ensure it stays aligned with your evolving values and priorities.

PART 2 ACHIEVABLE STEPS: CREATING A PERSONALIZED GROWTH ROADMAP

Think of achieving your goals as embarking on a carefully planned road trip. Without a map, even the most exciting journey can feel daunting or directionless. A personalized growth roadmap serves as your guide, breaking down the long road ahead into clear, achievable steps. It's not just about knowing your destination, it's about understanding the route, the landmarks along the way, and the tools you need to get there. This kind of structure transforms even the biggest ambitions into manageable, motivating progress, ensuring you move forward with confidence and clarity.

The initial step in creating your roadmap is to break your goal into smaller, actionable tasks. View each task as a building block essential to constructing your dream. Start with the big picture: What is your ultimate goal? From there, work backward, identifying the smaller tasks that will lead you there. Organizing these tasks by priority ensures that you visualize what matters most first. Techniques like prioritization matrices or simple task lists can help you determine which steps need immediate attention and which can wait. Celebrate short-term milestones along the way, whether it's completing a course, submitting a proposal, or carving out 15 minutes each day for focused work. Each milestone serves as a checkpoint, reminding you of how far you've come and fueling your momentum for the next phase.

Accountability is the compass that keeps you from drifting off course. Progress tracking tools, such as journals, habit trackers, or apps, give you a tangible way to document your journey. Record not only your achievements but also your setbacks and reflections, as these moments of learning are just as important as moments of triumph. Partnering with a friend, mentor, or accountability group can also keep you grounded. Share your roadmap with someone who believes in your vision, they'll provide encouragement, fresh perspectives, and, when needed, gentle nudges to keep you moving forward. Together, these systems help transform fleeting intentions into steady habits.

As you navigate your roadmap, regular reflection ensures you're still headed in the right direction. Life is unpredictable, and your goals might evolve with time. Set aside moments, monthly or quarterly, to evaluate your progress. Ask yourself questions like, "Am I still on track?" or "Have my priorities shifted?" Celebrate the milestones you've reached and use any missteps as learning opportunities to refine your approach. Adjust timelines or even reshape your goals if necessary. Flexibility is key; your roadmap should grow with you, serving as a dynamic guide rather than a fixed path. By embracing this adaptability, you ensure that every adjustment strengthens your journey, keeping you aligned with what truly matters to you.

Ultimately, a growth roadmap is more than a plan, it's a promise to yourself. It's a way to stay motivated, focused, and resilient, even when the road gets bumpy. By breaking down your dreams into achievable steps, tracking your progress, and staying open to change, you're not just chasing your goals, you're building the life you've always envisioned, one milestone at a time.

PART 3 CELEBRATING MILESTONES: ACKNOWLEDGING PROGRESS AND SUCCESS

Daydream about the moment you reach a milestone, a point on your journey where effort, persistence, and determination converge into a tangible success. It's not just a fleeting victory; it's an opportunity to pause, reflect, and acknowledge how far you've come. Celebrating these moments is about more than rewarding yourself, it's about solidifying the habits, choices, and resilience that led to your progress. Taking time to honor your achievements can be transformative, boosting your confidence, rekindling your motivation, and reminding you of your potential. Each celebration becomes a firm foundation, reinforcing your commitment to growth and energizing you for the next chapter of your journey.

Celebrating milestones can be deeply personal, and finding meaningful ways to honor them ensures the moment resonates. This could be as simple as treating yourself to an experience you love, a hike in nature, a favorite meal, or a relaxing evening unplugged from daily stresses. Small rewards like a book you've wanted to read, a new outfit, or even an afternoon off can feel symbolic, representing the dedication and work you've poured into your goal. Beyond personal rewards, sharing your achievements with others adds an element of connection and joy. Whether you choose to toast with close friends, write a heartfelt social media post, or share the story with a mentor, involving others in your celebration strengthens your sense of community. It's a way to say, "Look what we've done together", highlighting not only your efforts but also the support systems that made it possible.

Expressing gratitude for the journey that brought you to each milestone amplifies the joy of your achievement. Gratitude shifts your vision from what's still ahead to what's already been accomplished, anchoring you in the present. Take a moment to reflect on the obstacles you've overcome, the lessons learned, and the people who helped along the way. Gratitude journaling can be a particularly meaningful practice here. Write about what this milestone means to you, noting not only the accomplishment itself but also the personal growth and relationships that supported it. By putting these reflections into words, you create a lasting record of your progress, one you can revisit for encouragement during future challenges. Equally important, express appreciation to those who supported you, whether they offered advice, encouragement, or simply believed in you. Gratitude strengthens these relationships and reminds you that success is often a shared journey.

After the celebration, take time to recalibrate and set your sights on what comes next. Milestones are not endpoints; they are signposts marking your progress along the road to a larger vision. Reflection is key here, ask yourself meaningful questions like, "What did I learn from this experience?" and "What new opportunities does this open up for me?" Use these reflections to identify areas where you want to continue growing or entirely new paths you want to explore. Setting fresh goals keeps the momentum alive, challenging you to build on your success and stretch toward new horizons. Treat this process of reflection and goal setting as a celebration in its own right, a recognition of your ongoing commitment to personal and professional growth.

Celebrating milestones, big or small, is about honoring your journey. It's a reminder that every step forward is worth acknowledging, no matter how far you still want to go. By rewarding yourself meaningfully, expressing gratitude, and using each success as a springboard for the future, you create a rhythm of progress that inspires you to keep striving. These celebrations are more than moments of joy; they are moments of transformation, reaffirming your purpose and your belief in what's possible.

PART 4 MAINTAINING MOMENTUM: STAYING MOTIVATED ON YOUR JOURNEY

Sustaining motivation over the course of a long journey can feel challenging, but with the right mindset and strategies, it becomes not only manageable but deeply rewarding. One of the most impactful ways to stay energized is through visualization. Close your eyes and envision yourself achieving your goals, not as distant fantasies but as tangible realities. Reflect upon the pride on your face, the sense of accomplishment in your heart, and the joy of realizing your efforts have paid off. Summon those doors that success opens and the possibilities that follow. Regularly engaging in this practice, whether in the morning to set the tone for your day or at night as you reflect, can help anchor you to your "why" and reignite the passion that fuels your progress.

Another cornerstone of maintaining momentum is incorporating self-care into your routine. It's easy to fall into the trap of pushing yourself endlessly in the pursuit of your goals, but neglecting rest and renewal only leads to burnout. Self-care isn't an indulgence; it's an essential part of the process. Take intentional breaks to rejuvenate your mind and body. Whether it's a brisk walk outdoors, a calming yoga session, or simply savoring a few moments of quiet with a cup of tea, these pauses act as reset points. They allow you to recharge and return to your work with greater enthusiasm and creativity. Embracing mindfulness during these moments further enhances their restorative power. Pause to breathe deeply, immerse yourself in the present, and let go of mental clutter. This balance between effort and rest creates the steady rhythm needed for sustained progress.

No journey is without its twists and turns, and setbacks are a natural part of the process. When challenges arise, they can feel discouraging, but with a resilient mindset, they become opportunities for growth. Approach obstacles with curiosity rather than frustration, reframing them as puzzles to solve rather than walls to climb. Ask yourself reflective questions like, "What can I learn from this?" or "What's one small step I can take to move forward?" By adopting this perspective, you shift your fixation from the problem itself to actionable solutions. Leaning on your support network during these moments can also make a significant difference. Reach out to mentors, peers, or trusted friends for advice or encouragement. Their insights and experiences can provide fresh perspectives that light the way through even the toughest challenges.

Celebrating progress, no matter how small, keeps the motivation alive and the journey fulfilling. Every step forward deserves acknowledgment, as it represents growth and effort. Cultivate a habit of recognizing and honoring these wins, whether by journaling about them or speaking affirmations aloud. For example, at the end of each day, take a moment to say, "I'm proud of the effort I made today, no matter how small it seems." These affirmations serve as powerful reminders of your abilities and reinforce your belief in your capacity to succeed. Journaling, too, can be a profound motivator. Documenting your achievements and reflecting on how far you've come creates a visible record of progress, one you can revisit when motivation wanes. This practice not only tracks your journey but reminds you of the resilience and dedication that have carried you through.

Ultimately, staying motivated is about finding joy in the process and celebrating the journey as much as the destination. By visualizing your success, caring for your well-being, reframing obstacles, and acknowledging your wins, you create a sustainable rhythm that propels you forward. Momentum isn't about constant motion, it's about balance, reflection, and consistent steps that keep you moving in the direction of your dreams.

PART 5 EMBRACING CHANGE: ADAPTING AND THRIVING IN LIFE'S TRANSITIONS

Life unfolds in unexpected ways, presenting us with challenges, opportunities, and moments that push us outside of our comfort zones. Change can feel unsettling, stirring up uncertainty and fear, but it is also one of life's greatest teachers. When you view change through the lens of opportunity, it becomes a powerful force for transformation. Instead of focusing on what is lost or unknown, shift your perspective to what can be gained. Change is not an end but a beginning, a chance to grow, to discover new strengths, and to evolve. By embracing it, you open yourself to possibilities that may lead to fulfillment you never imagined.

Thriving amidst change begins with resilience, the ability to recover, adapt, and thrive in the face of adversity. Resilience isn't something you're born with; it's a skill that can be developed through consistent practice. Start by cultivating a positive outlook. When challenges arise, reframe them as opportunities for growth. Ask yourself, "What can I learn from this?" or "How can I use this experience to build my strength?" Developing problem-solving skills is another critical component. Break challenges into smaller, manageable parts and center on actionable steps. Resilience doesn't mean avoiding difficulty; it means meeting it head-on, confident in your ability to adapt and move forward.

Equally important is cultivating a mindset that welcomes change. Flexibility and openness are essential tools for navigating life's transitions. Start by letting go of rigid expectations about how things "should" be. Instead, embrace a more adaptable approach, one that allows you to adjust your goals as circumstances shift. Flexible goal-setting involves creating objectives that align with your core values but remain adaptable to changing situations. For example, rather than saying, "I must achieve this by next year," reframe it as "I will pursue this goal while remaining open to new opportunities along the way." This adaptability not only reduces stress but also creates room for innovation and unexpected break-throughs.

Reframing setbacks as teachable moments is another powerful way to thrive during transitions. When challenges arise, they often feel like roadblocks. However, with the right mindset, they can become valuable opportunities for self-discovery. Instead of asking, "Why is this happening to me?" ask, "What can this teach me?" or "How can I grow from this experience?" This approach helps you see adversity as a tool for growth rather than a barrier. Each setback becomes a lesson, each challenge a chance to strengthen your resilience and adaptability.

Real-life stories often illustrate the transformative power of embracing change. Emily, for instance, faced a crossroads when she left her corporate career to pursue a passion for environmental advocacy. Initially overwhelmed by uncertainty, she turned to mentorship and support from peers who had navigated similar transitions. With a positive mindset and a willingness to adapt,

Emily discovered talents she didn't know she possessed, ultimately creating a fulfilling and impactful career. Similarly, Mark found himself forced to make a career shift after his industry downsized. Though the change was unexpected, he saw it as an opportunity to explore digital marketing, a field he'd always been curious about. By embracing the challenge and remaining flexible in his goals, he not only built a new skill set but also found a career path that aligned with his passions and strengths.

Your own life transitions are opportunities to grow into the person you are meant to become. When change comes, remind yourself that it is a natural part of life, a force that propels you forward, even when the path feels uncertain. Embrace change with curiosity and approach each transition with the belief that it holds the potential to lead you to something greater. Cultivate resilience through positivity and problem-solving and remain open to the unexpected. Life's greatest adventures often begin where your comfort zone ends. Let change be your ally, guiding you toward a life rich in growth, learning, and possibility.

A Note of Gratitude and an Invitation to Share

Thank you for allowing this book to be a part of your journey. It has been my hope that the words within these pages have inspired you, challenged you, and reminded you of your own incredible power to grow, transform, and shine. As you close this chapter and continue crafting the life you deserve, I'd like to ask one final favor: if this book has touched your heart, sparked a meaningful change, or offered you tools to thrive, would you consider sharing your experience with others?

Your voice has the power to inspire someone else who might be standing where you once were—unsure, searching, and ready for a sign. By leaving a review on Amazon, you can help this message reach those who need it most. Your thoughts don't just reflect your journey; they create ripples of encouragement, helping others take that first brave step toward a more empowered life.

PAY IT FORWARD

If you feel compelled, I'd love to hear how this book has impacted your life. Did it give you a tool you needed, a perspective that shifted, or an affirmation that lifted your spirit? By sharing your story, you light the way for someone else to begin theirs.

As a small token of inspiration, let me leave you with this thought:

> "The meaning of life is to find your gift. The purpose of life is to give it away."
>
> PABLO PICASSO

Your review is a gift—one that could inspire another to uncover their own strength, find clarity in their struggles, or take a leap they've been too afraid to make.

Thank you for paying forward what you've learned and for being part of this shared journey of growth and empowerment. Your words, just like your actions, have the power to create meaningful change.

With gratitude and admiration,

Zara Imani

For Review Link Click Hereor use this QR Code!

Conclusion

As you pause to reflect on this transformative journey, take a moment to appreciate how far you've come. This book has been more than just a guide, it has been a companion, walking beside you as you unearth the vibrant, empowered life that's always been within your reach. Together, we've delved deep into the layers of self-doubt, exposing its roots in limiting beliefs and dismantling the patterns that once held you back. Along the way, you've cultivated tools and insights to replace those doubts with self-belief, self-compassion, and a renewed sense of purpose.

You've confronted and reshaped the narratives that defined you. Through self-reflection, you've uncovered your authentic self, a self that thrives not by conforming to external expectations but by embracing its uniqueness. Vulnerability, once viewed as a weakness, has become your strength, a gateway to deeper connection and unwavering authenticity. You've realigned with your core values, giving voice to your innermost truths and desires, and discovered the immense power of living a life that resonates with who you truly are.

The journey didn't stop with self-discovery. You've crafted a personalized self-care plan, recognizing that nurturing your mind, body, and spirit is not an indulgence but a foundation for growth. You've learned to weave mindfulness into the fabric of your daily life, turning ordinary moments into sacred acts of presence and gratitude. You've established boundaries that protect your energy, and you've sought out a supportive community, understanding the profound impact of surrounding yourself with people who uplift and inspire.

The transformation you've embarked upon is both inspiring and tangible. It's no longer about surviving the doubts and fears that once defined you, it's about thriving. You've stepped into a life of intentionality, guided by clarity, self-awareness, and resilience. This journey has illuminated a vital truth: self-doubt is not an unconquerable force. Through authenticity, determination, and a commitment to growth, you've proven that you hold the power to rewrite your story.

Now, the path forward lies in taking what you've learned and infusing it into every aspect of your life. Action is the bridge between insight and transformation. Begin with small, intentional steps: start your mornings with affirmations that ground you in self-belief, pause for moments of mindfulness that connect you to the present, and engage with communities that fuel your growth. Set goals that align with your values and let your vision board serve as a daily reminder of your aspirations. Every small action you take propels you closer to the life you've envisioned.

Empowerment is not a destination; it's a lifelong journey. Each day is an opportunity to learn, grow, and shine brighter. Celebrate your victories, no matter how small, and view setbacks not as failures, but as the path of progress. Your life is your masterpiece, and you hold the brush. Each decision, each moment of courage, adds color and texture to the canvas of your reality.

The future stretches before you, brimming with possibilities. Continue to seek out resources that inspire and challenge you. Participate in workshops, join online communities, and connect with mentors who align with your vision. Surround yourself with individuals who celebrate your authenticity and encourage your evolution. Keep exploring, keep growing, and never stop reaching for the best version of yourself.

Let me leave you with a final affirmation to carry forward:

> *"I am the architect of my life; I build its foundation and choose its contents."*

Let these words remind you of the incredible power you hold to shape your reality to create a life filled with purpose, joy, and fulfillment. You are capable, deserving, and ready to embrace the life you've always dreamed of.

Thank you for allowing me to accompany you on this transformative journey. Remember, the best version of yourself is always waiting just beyond hesitation, ready to shine boldly and confidently. Step forward, glow brightly, and make your life extraordinary. The world is waiting for your light. Now is the time to let it shine.

References

Success Part 0: The Psychology of Self-Doubt https://hiddenbrain.org/podcast/the-psychology-of-self-doubt/

Cognitive Restructuring Techniques for Reframing Thoughts https://positivepsychology.com/cbt-cognitive-restructuring-cognitive-distortions/

Affirmations and Neuroplasticity https://www.psychologytoday.com/us/blog/anxiety-another-name-pain/202001/affirmations-and-neuroplasticity

9 Women in Tech Share Their Stories About Imposter ... https://builtin.com/articles/9-women-tech-share-their-stories-about-imposter-syndrome

Research https://brenebrown.com/the-research/

Understanding the Importance of Embracing Your True Self ... https://quenza.com/blog/embracing-your-true-self/

Confronting the Fear of Being Judged: A Step-by- ... https://www.addrc.org/confronting-the-fear-of-being-judged-a-step-by-step-approach/

The neuropsychology of self-reflection in psychiatric illness https://pmc.ncbi.nlm.nih.gov/articles/PMC4022422/

Self-Care Isn't Selfish: 17 Tips for Making Yourself a Priority https://health.clevelandclinic.org/why-self-care-isnt-selfish-advice-for-women

The Ultimate Guide to Holistic Wellness for Busy Women https://bohobloomprintables.com/the-ultimate-guide-to-holistic-wellness-for-busy-women/

How to Stop Feeling Guilty about Practicing Self-Care https://psychcentral.com/blog/how-to-stop-feeling-guilty-about-practicing-self-care

Mindfulness exercises https://www.mayoclinic.org/healthy-lifestyle/consumer-health/in-depth/mindfulness-exercises/art-20046356

The Importance of Personal Boundaries - Psych Central https://psychcentral.com/relationships/the-importance-of-personal-boundaries

3 Assertive Communication Techniques to Earn the ... https://melodywilding.com/3-assertive-communication-techniques-to-earn-the-respect-you-deserve/

How to Set Boundaries , Examples and Scripts https://momentumpsychology.com/how-to-set-boundaries-examples-and-scripts/

6 Ways to Set Boundaries Without Guilt | Psychology Today https://www.psychologytoday.com/us/blog/conquering-codependency/202208/6-ways-set-boundaries-without-guilt

The Power of Community in Personal Growth https://medium.com/hello-love/the-

power-of-community-in-personal-growth-a-comprehensive-guide-
cf6a518f539a

14 Tips to Find Like-Minded People (Who Understand You) https://socialself.com/blog/
find-like-minded/

Perceived Benefits of Online Support Groups for Women ... https://www.tandfonline.
com/doi/full/10.1080/03630240903238719

Creating Safe Spaces for Courageous Conversations https://www.sagethinking.com.au/
resources/articles/on-leadership/creating-safe-spaces-for-courageous-conver
sations/

Fixed Mindset vs. Growth Mindset Examples https://biglifejournal.com/blogs/blog/
fixed-mindset-vs-growth-mindset-examples?srsltid=AfmBOopbYvy
TOsa64Retxx57Gc_JvCP7e9nlZ0nVsJDXTzdRARTc0Mgr

10 Ways to Overcome Perfectionism – Oregon Counseling https://oregoncounseling.
com/article/10-ways-to-overcome-perfectionism/

Famous Failures: 23 Stories to Inspire You to Succeed https://www.bradaronson.com/
famous-failures/

4 Steps to Overcome Negative Thoughts https://mindfulness.com/mindful-living/over
come-negative-thoughts

The Benefits of Mindfulness for Women's Health https://www.promotingwomen
shealth.com/blog/the-benefits-of-mindfulness-for-womens-health.html

Mindfulness + Meditation Resources | Stanford Health Library https://healthlibrary.stan
ford.edu/books-resources/mindfulness-meditation.html

The 4 Best Meditation Apps of 2024 | Reviews by Wirecutter https://www.nytimes.com/
wirecutter/reviews/best-meditation-apps/

What is Mindful Self-Compassion? (Incl. Exercises + PDF) https://positivepsychology.
com/mindful-self-compassion/

How To Make A Vision Board And What to Include - BetterUp https://www.betterup.
com/blog/how-to-create-vision-board

Aligning Your Values With Your Goals Assures Inner Success https://medium.com/@
amisiga/aligning-your-values-with-your-goals-assures-inner-success-
ef0729ce4448

Mastering Long-Term Motivation: Key Strategies for Success https://medium.com/@
francesco.saviano87/mastering-long-term-motivation-essential-strategies-for-
success-b539d44e5bc1

Heroines Journey Stories to Inspire You https://www.thesophiawomensinstitute.com/
heroines-journey-stories